THE ENIGMA OF

Giorgio de Chirico

By the same author

Beyond the Lighthouse

Colette: The Difficulty of Loving

Jean Cocteau

Louise of Stolberg

Piaf

Raymond Radiguet

Sade's Wife

Simone de Beauvoir: The Woman and Her Work

Anthologies

Cocteau's World

My Contemporaries (Jean Cocteau)

The Leather Jacket (Cesare Pavese)

The Passionate Philosopher (Marquis de Sade)

Selected Letters: The Marquis de Sade

Translations

Giorgio de Chirico: *Hebdomeros*; *The Memoirs of Giorgio de Chirico*

Jean Cocteau: *Le Livre Blanc*; *Opium*

Colette: *Duo and Le Toutounier*; *The Other Woman*; *Retreat from Love*

Marquis de Sade: *Crimes of Love*; *The Gothic Tales of the Marquis de Sade*; *The Mystified Magistrate*

Cesare Pavese: *Selected Poems*

Edith Piaf: My *Life*

Emile Zola: *Earth*

Margaret Crosland

THE ENIGMA OF
Giorgio de Chirico

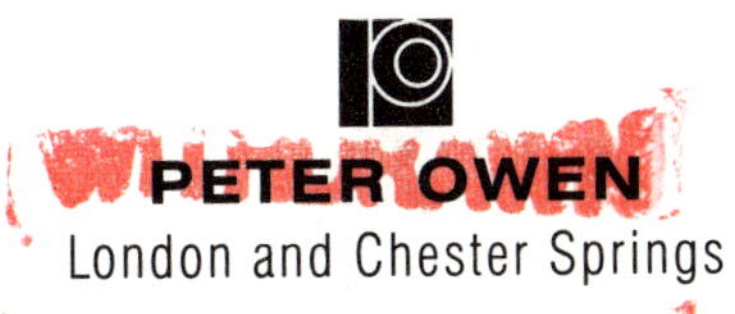

PETER OWEN
London and Chester Springs

PETER OWEN PUBLISHERS
73 Kenway Road, London SW5 0RE
Peter Owen books are distributed in the USA by Dufour Editions Inc.,
Chester Springs, PA 19425-0007

First published in Great Britain 1999

A catalogue record for this book is available from the British Library

ISBN 0 7206 1042 7

Printed in Great Britain by Hillman Printers (Frome) Ltd

Preface

FOR the first time in my life I have found myself writing an unauthorized and consciously personal biography. Ever since I could remember I had known the works of de Chirico the painter, but when, thanks to Jean Cocteau and his *The Lay Mystery* of 1928, I first read that intriguing surrealist novel *Hebdomeros*, published the following year, de Chirico the writer took me into a new world. Then, after reading his *Memoirs* of 1945 and 1962, I began to wonder why he had left so much out. I set myself the task of finding out.

First of all I spent a few complicated years studying the neglected area of dual-media expression – visual and written – in de Chirico's work; then I finally embarked on a biography of this elusive person, soon realizing that there was no escape from those key terms in the titles of the early paintings: mystery, melancholy, enigma.

In fact those three words could apply to the response I received from Italy: a response of silence. It was assumed, I supposed, that there was nothing more to be said; the policy of the family was to say nothing. So I decided that I would carry out what research I could and, for better or worse, add – cautiously – my own interpretation whenever I thought, rightly or wrongly, that I had made a discovery. I *did* discover the story of de Chirico's first marriage, which he did not mention in his *Memoirs*: his second wife had threatened to kill herself if he did. I realized at the same time how relationships with women, beginning with his mother, influenced the content of his painting over the years. More evidence came to light too about the methods de Chirico used, in the late 1920s especially, in order to paint quickly and how he was not averse to producing works in the style of early paintings and predating them.

Biography is, technically, 'a written account of the life of an individual', and autobiography is no different, in principle, except that the individual and the writer are the same person. In 1944 George Orwell made a savage comment on the genre in a piece he wrote apropos *The Secret Life of Salvador Dalí*. 'Autobiography', he said, 'is only to be trusted when it reveals something disgraceful. A man who gives a good account of himself is probably lying, since any life when viewed from the inside is simply a series of defeats.' Some fifty years later John Sturrock wrote in *The Language of Autobiography* that the genre represents 'an effort made by those who write at the integration of their past lives and present selves: the autobiographer wishes to stand forth in print in the form of a whole'. Orwell believed that even a 'flagrantly dishonest' book, like the autobiographical writings of Frank Harris, can unintentionally give a true picture of the author. De Chirico was not flagrantly dishonest, but in his selective way – with all his mystery, melancholy, enigma and, it must be said, anger – he proved both Orwell and Sturrock to be right. Italy had already produced two impressive autobiographers, Benvenuto Cellini and Vittorio Alfieri, both highly readable but far from accurate; the enhanced self-told life story was something of an Italian genre.

At the approach to the millennium, it is not so much those who write their own stories who reveal 'something disgraceful' but those who write the stories of others, since biographical success with the public is often judged by the quantity and degree of 'disgrace' discovered. There is little of that here, only an attempt to follow the career of an independent, complex man who hoped that he could express his personal and philosophical preoccupations by painting for some eighty years – painting what he liked and how he liked, repainting old works if he wanted to and even denouncing some of his own paintings as fakes if he chose to. At the same time he relentlessly attacked 'modern' art and the surrealism which had been so deeply influenced by his own early work. His life is constantly interesting to any student of the creative forces.

If I cannot thank his nephew and niece for any cooperation, I take pleasure in the indirect help I have received from the imaginative writings of his younger brother, Alberto Savinio, which often gave me insight into Giorgio de Chirico's approach to life and work.

The list of other helpful people is long: Rhoda Poetzl Billingsley in Rome, Denise Merlin in Paris, Gene Simpson in Toronto. In Britain, J.G. Ballard, Josephine Balmer, Stephen Byrne, Roger Cardinal, Adrian Daintrey, June Daventry, William Feaver, Antonia Owen, Nancy Pickford, Elfreda Powell, Nina Rootes, Jeffrey Simmons and especially Adriana Hubbard and Christopher Crofton-Sleigh. Also the Tate Gallery, Wildenstein and Co. Ltd, the London Library, the University of London Library, the county libraries of Kent, East Sussex and West Sussex, the Italian Bookshop, London, the Italian Cultural Institute and the Institut de France.

For help with typescripts and disks, I am grateful to Eleanor and Guy Coleman, Wendy Mackenzie and Christopher Crofton-Sleigh.

The extract from Geoffrey Grigson's 'The New Dummy' from *The Harp of Aeolus* (published by Routledge) is reproduced by courtesy of David Higham Associates.

Margaret Crosland

Contents

List of Illustrations

between pages 66 and 67

1
The Child's Brain

THE 1914 painting *The Child's Brain,* which now hangs in the Moderna Museet in Stockholm, is one of the best known of de Chirico's early works. It measures 81.3 cm by 64.8 cm and cannot be described as decorative, but no image in the painter's vast output is more significant in any exploration of his life and work, and none had more influence on the early development of surrealism. The histories of the man who painted it and of the man who some five years later bought it and then owned it for most of his life, André Breton, symbolize what happened when the nineteenth century eventually ended, after its life had been prolonged until 1914.

Breton had realized the creative importance of the unconscious mind in artistic creation and sensed that de Chirico proved, unconsciously, the value of Freud's explorations concerning dreams in the treatment of mental illness. He bought the painting. De Chirico, however, was interested in philosophy, not psychology, and before two decades had passed the two men had become enemies. Sadly, perhaps, this changed situation forms an essential part of the enigmatic de Chirico story.

One of the earliest known photographs of Giorgio de Chirico as a child shows him wearing the pleated skirt and black cap of a Greek evzone, staring at the camera with the fixed, expressionless gaze made necessary by the state of photography at the time. He was born in Volos, Greece, on 10 July 1888. His family were living there because the Barone Evaristo de Chirico, the boy's father, was an experienced railway engineer and had been made responsible for the construction of an important new railway line linking the capital, Athens, with Salonika, the capital of Thessaly, in the north. It is still one of the most important railways in Greece. Volos, on the north side of the gulf of Volos, was roughly halfway between the two cities that were to be linked.

Evaristo de Chirico was not typical of the old aristocratic family into which he had been born. The family had originally lived in the Terra di Lavoro, in western Italy, and the name 'Chirico' was first mentioned in documents of the mid fifteenth century. They then moved to Sicily, where they remained during the eighteenth and early nineteenth centuries. This information was published by Giorgio's younger brother, Andrea (who had adopted the name Alberto Savinio), in 1937. The family ancestors included an archbishop who was buried in Palermo Cathedral, while another member of the family entered the army, distinguishing himself as a captain in a regiment of bombardiers and also during an epidemic of cholera. Maria Theresa, the empress of Austria, rewarded him with the *particule nobiliaire*, and the family could then style themselves 'de Chirico'. Savinio also noted that his grandfather had served the King of Sardinia before and during that country's entry into the Kingdom of Italy.

Giorgio's father had apparently trained in Tuscany and Turin and was said to have been a member of some international professional organizations. He was surely an unusual man in one way, because he was the only member of a large aristocratic family who showed any desire to work, to use his brain. As it happened, he may have been the only one capable of work, for his brothers and sisters were at the least highly eccentric. 'Uncle and Aunt mad,' wrote Cocteau in 1928, adding a few more details that he may have heard from the painter's brother in Paris but not attempting to describe the whole family. Alberto Savinio may have enhanced the stories he told about his unusual relatives, but he surely did not invent all the details, even if he sometimes changed a Christian name.

Both de Chirico brothers seem to have been relatively close to their father's youngest brother, Gustavo – or Gaetano, as Savinio called him. Later in life Giorgio even wrote a poem 'Sur la mort de mon oncle'. This is not a great poem, but it can be linked with the mood of his early painting, for it tells how his uncle seemed to be living in a prison, his life passing slowly in a silent room. Indeed, the existence of Gustavo/Gaetano had been strange from the beginning, even for those times, when so many people lived in claustrophobic conditions. As a little boy, at the age when most children spent their time in violent exercise or in play related to 'war and killing activities more deeply natural to men', he had passed his days sitting on a stool at his mother's feet working at embroidery. Apparently he might have married a Dutch heiress, but she was a Protestant and refused to be converted to 'popery'. However, Alberto Savinio suspected that the match failed because Gustavo had been too deeply influenced by his mother. (She was not the only dominating mother in the de Chirico family, as became obvious later.)

This uncle, who never did marry, later became a Catholic bigot and was excessively sensitive to cold. Savinio remembered him as an elderly man living in Florence and wearing several old jackets one on top of another in order to keep warm. He never opened any windows, and his apartment smelt like a sickroom. One old servant, Annunciata, remained to him, and they competed in who would attend mass and vespers the more often. Their sins would not allow them to enter paradise, but whoever won this competition would end in purgatory.

Gustavo suffered from chronic stomach trouble and received a special dispensation from the Pope allowing him to eat grilled meat during the Friday fast. He claimed that he read Dante, but the bookmark always remained at the same page. He particularly hated the 'modern' work of the contemporary religious novelist Antonio Fogazzaro, though he had never read it, and he equated modernism with 'heresy, atheism, Protestantism', for Protestants were not Christians. Later his nephew Giorgio, who was also plagued with stomach troubles, could not condemn 'modernism' fiercely enough. He may have learned something from his unusual uncle.

Giorgio also saw what it was like to live in genteel but still eccentric poverty. His uncle had been kept alive by a small allowance from his sister Agläé, a wealthy widow, but as time passed its value had dwindled. Since the house was now full of empty bedrooms, Gustavo thought he might earn a little money by renting them out for one lira a night – but only to impoverished elderly women well known in the parish for their genuine religious beliefs. However, his aristocratic background made it impossible for him to answer a knock at the door, and if his old servant was out the door remained closed. When Andrea de Chirico could not gain admittance one day he went to find a locksmith, only to discover, once the door was opened, that his uncle was standing behind it shivering with fear.

Aunt Agläé, the wealthy widow, had been married twice: first to a banker and then to the Marchés Afan de Rivera, a Spanish grandee. She had devised a special way of passing the time, at least at night. When everyone was asleep she would get up from bed, put on a ball-gown and elbow-length black gloves, light all the lamps in the drawing-room and greet the dawn while reading the letters of Madame de Sévigné. Her first husband, the banker, had left her an inheritance which helped to support her brother, though after her death most of her fortune went to the church.

There were three other sisters. Zenaide, who was remembered as being very beautiful and majestic, married a captain in the French garrison of the papal guard and courageously accompanied him when he was sent to fight brigands in the countryside. Once when she entered an embassy on her husband's arm she so impressed the waiting officials that the orchestra immediately struck up the national anthem. Apollonia – or Olympe, as Cocteau chose to call her – had a most distressing habit: she would kneel down on the floor, loosen her hair, and rub her head along the sofa. Eventually she became bald and had to wear a toupee. Of Olga, the last sister, nothing is known.

There was also one more brother, Alberto, described by his nephew Savinio, who chose the same Christian name for his professional life, as 'tall, handsome, elegant, very much the *seigneur*'. He was obviously sophisticated; he painted with 'feminine diligence' seascapes and portraits and wrote 'perfectly chaste love poems in French' and set them to music. He also played the piano 'with taste and feeling'. There was a rumour in the family that Alberto had wanted to marry Giorgio's mother, Gemma Cervetto, but she had chosen Evaristo de Chirico instead. His love of the sea led him to leave Florence for Livorno, but by the time he had reached his thirties the family eccentricity had taken over – he never left the house any more and could only watch the sea through the window. His nephew said that he was a kind of Narcissus, with a moustache and long side-whiskers. Like nearly all the members of this family he had his phobias: he was so afraid he might fall through a hole in the floor that he never moved from one room to another without pushing a chair in front of him. He also sealed up all the windows in his own apartment and in the one below. It seems strange that so many members of this family wanted to cut themselves off from ordinary life. What were they frightened of?

The eccentricity did not start with Evaristo's generation: it had existed earlier. The mother of this large family had been Spanish, the Countess Mabili y Buligny, daughter of the consul in Corfu who acted for His Catholic Majesty the King of Spain. As a young girl of sixteen she was so beautiful that she attracted the attention of the Barone Giorgio C. (Savinio's term), who was then ambassador to the King of Sardinia, while on his way to Constantinople. He at once asked her parents for her hand, and they were married a month later. Like most members of this extraordinary family she had unorthodox views of her own. She would not allow her portrait to be painted, for she was convinced that if a portrait existed she herself would not – she would fade away and die. However, she remained a devout Catholic, and when she fell in love with a handsome young officer in the Sardinian navy she knew she must atone for her 'sin'. She therefore gave up the greatest pleasure in her life – the pleasure of eating macaroni. When she was eighty-two she told her confessor the whole story, and he at once released her from her vow of self-punishment. 'The next day', wrote Savinio, 'she ate so much macaroni that she died.' Nobody in the de Chirico family ever did things by halves. Cocteau was to remark in 1928 that 'Such antecedents contribute to remove any picturesque character from de Chirico's work.' With the exception of Gustavo, the painter himself mentioned none of these strange but fascinating people.

Evaristo de Chirico had no time to be 'picturesque' or eccentric. He was too busy, too responsible, too interested in his sons. In the family photographs the bearded Barone looks more like a grandfather than a father, and in fact his elder son, who admired him deeply, described him as 'a man of the nineteenth century', a 'gentleman of olden times, courageous, loyal, hardworking, intelligent and good'. He had talents which both his sons inherited: 'he drew, had a good ear for music, had gifts of observation and irony. He also hated injustice, loved animals, treated the rich and powerful in a lofty manner, and was always ready to help the weak and the poor.' But, like so many men of the nineteenth century, he was so prudish that topics such as childbirth could not be mentioned even in adult company, and he was so overprotective of his sons that they were not allowed to ride bicycles. Weapons could not be mentioned either – apart from cannon, for they were not usually kept in houses. However, the courageous Barone had once been injured in a duel, and his wife had carefully preserved the bullet which had been removed from his body. Other surprisingly unmentionable subjects included disinfectants and microbes, and Giorgio was quickly removed from a Catholic lycée when, like every schoolboy, he began picking up bad language.

Life in Volos had more serious dangers, for the town was subject to violent storms and frequent, if minor, earthquakes. (Later, however, in 1954 and 1955, two of them were so disastrous that many buildings, including the museum, were destroyed.) When Giorgio was young the town also suffered from aggressive Turkish raiding parties. Turkey had lost Thessaly to Greece in 1881 but wanted it back so badly that its soldiers succeeded in occupying Volos for a time in 1897. The Turks committed various murders, and news of these reached the children. Many of the inhabitants moved out of the town, while others practised firing rifles at a shooting-range. The raiders would have destroyed the railway line if de Chirico senior had not struggled to save it, later receiving the Order of St George as a reward.

Yet Volos also possessed its own magic; life in this ancient maritime town 'was full of metaphysical and provincial events'. Later Giorgio wrote nostalgically of fishing trips at dawn over the mirror-smooth sea, and his brother told more imaginatively in his 1943 book *Casa 'La Vita'* that the gods often came to Volos, especially in the morning. Mercury would fly down unexpectedly in his gleaming chariot, and his winged feet would touch the rooftops before he leaped away again. Volos was thought to be the site of the ancient Iolcus from where the Argonauts set sail in search of the Golden Fleece. Giorgio said that he never saw anything more beautiful than Greece and admitted that he would never be able to transpose its particular quality into painting. He had his first sight of athletes, later to appear in his work, while watching the first modern Olympic Games in Athens in 1896, but he was bored by a performance of *Iphigenia in Tauris*, mainly because it took place in the open air. He had forgotten, perhaps, that Euripides had known no other theatre.

The young Andrea de Chirico had been born in Athens in 1891, when the family were living there temporarily. His birth compensated for the loss of the eldest child, Adèle, who had died when she was about six. His elder brother had 'a confused memory of him', and looking back he saw him 'as small, disturbingly small, like certain alarming people one sees in dreams'. But Andrea was not alarming. 'My brother was the handsome one of the family,' wrote Giorgio, 'and our mother was very proud of him. She made him wear big lace collars which stood out against his dark blue jacket.' She would also say that 'he looked like a portrait by Van Dyck'. Every morning the entire domestic staff carried out the elaborate ritual of curling his hair into long ringlets, after which his mother proudly took the little boy for 'a walk along the avenue with the pepper-trees', where he was admired by old women servants sitting on the benches. The couple were greeted with cries of '*pulachimu*' – 'my little bird' – and women would spit after him to bring him luck.

Andrea hardly seemed to need their good wishes; his vocation for music – only his first vocation, as it turned out – developed early, and whereas Giorgio soon gave up playing the cello, in which he was not very interested, Andrea went to the Conservatoire of Music in Athens, where he was so precocious that he was awarded diplomas in piano playing and composition by the time he was twelve.

The boys' father did all he could to give both boys the best education available; he encouraged Giorgio's drawing from the moment his son showed a propensity for it, at the age of about eight, engaging drawing-masters and general tutors for him and finally sending him to the Athens Polytechnic around 1903 (when he was fifteen). In his *Memoirs*, de Chirico described in detail the type of work he did in the fine-arts department there – much drawing and copying, which he had been doing at home for years; much work in black and white – and told how he learned painfully that oil painting was done with linseed oil, not olive oil. He did not paint or draw from life until four years or so later, but he often walked out into the countryside on his own to paint landscapes. He also went to the harbour of Piraeus, the port of Athens, where he drew 'steamers and sailing ships and boats of all kinds'. Such images, especially glimpses of distant sails, were to appear in many of his paintings later, usually in unexpected and mysterious urban surroundings.

In middle age the painter remembered his early drawing-masters mostly with admiration, sometimes for the way in which they succeeded in living without money. They included a Greek, an Italian, and a Swiss-French artist called Gilleron who painted subjects from the ancient world – the Acropolis, ruins of temples and broken columns. There was also a portrait-painter, George Jacobides, who had previously worked at the Akademie der Bildenden Künste in Munich and may well have introduced his student to the German romantic painters.

What of the loving mother, Gemma de Chirico, the least documented, most mysterious member of the family? Her elder son said little about her in his *Memoirs*, where she appears as a conventional background figure, running her household with much help from servants. The only details about her come from the woman who was her daughter-in-law for a time, Giorgio's first wife, Raissa. Nothing was known about her family, but she was born in Genoa and may have had a Turkish mother or grandmother: Gemma and Evaristo were married in Constantinople. Raissa's theory was that she may have been a singer in a minor touring company performing operettas and possibly met her husband during his travels in the course of his work. Raissa based her assumption on the Baronessa's passion for jewellery (both genuine and fake), on her use of make-up and also on her mentality. But this daughter-in-law had had a good deal of theatrical experience herself and may have looked for this background on the basis of only slight evidence. Any such background would probably not have been mentioned because the aristocratic de Chirico family might have been embarrassed by what seemed an 'unsuitable' match. Gemma de Chirico never allowed her sons to forget her – Giorgio's portraits of her and Savinio's writing are proof of that – but her story remained a mystery to them.

In its way, this was an extended family, for there were two other members, at least for a time. Nicola, the cook, not only cooked, he nursed the family during an influenza epidemic, kept a pistol under his pillow in case he had to protect the family during his master's absences, arranged for the furniture to be taken out of the house when earthquakes threatened, played with the two boys and rescued them when they were attacked by tough little urchins from the town. The family could hardly have managed day-to-day life without him, and in this dependence on servants they were of course typical of the contemporary bourgeoisie. The other family member was Trollolò, a mongrel dog who had unexpectedly come to the door one night. The family were taken aback by the sound of what appeared to be an unexpected visitor: could this have been a Turkish enemy or a refugee? It was a refugee – though not a human one – and the pages in which de Chirico remembered his love for this affectionate and ingenious animal are more moving than any he wrote about a human being, at least in his *Memoirs*. Trollolò felt so close to the family that he would howl miserably when Giorgio's father was ill, upsetting the Baronessa but offering the only sympathy he could. Sadly the poor dog disappeared one year when the family for once did not take him on holiday with them. Giorgio maintained that he loved this animal more than any of the others did, and even in his middle age he felt a melancholy sense of loss when he thought of Trollolò.

This animal certainly stirred up deep emotions within the family, for in *Casa 'La Vita'* Andrea de Chirico turned the arrival and loss of the dog into a melodrama. In his piece named after the dog, the two brothers are given their real names, while his parents are given others. Andrea maintained that his father hated the animal, kicked him when nobody was looking and eventually got rid of him as a stray. He also maintained that *he* loved Trollolò more than anyone else did. Did this story indirectly reveal hidden tensions within the family? And why did Andrea choose to show such ambivalent feelings towards his father? The same collection also included a moving fantasy entitled 'My Mother Doesn't Understand Me', the whole story, written after her death, implying that *he* had not understood her and had not shown her any love. In this fantasy she appears as a little hen persistently calling out from an empty room in the house. When her son, in one of his many appearances as 'Nivasio Dolcemare' in his own work, finally understands what she is expressing, she falls silent. Like everything written by Savinio it is sad and comical at the same time, and this was his way of dealing with his nostalgic love. How much truth is concealed behind the story is unclear, and perhaps in the end there is no obvious truth; the writing supplies a descant above the autobiographical melody. If Giorgio's descriptions of family life were 'straight', and written a long time after the events described, those written by his brother were imaginative, oblique and ironic. Both accounts contribute to the picture of an unusual family, where an appearance of normality concealed the creative potential of these two boys.

The family life, with its deeply contrasting scenes of Turkish raiders, idyllic fishing parties, earthquakes and classical ruins, was to come to an end, and the melancholy so prevalent in de Chirico's early painting crept into everyday existence. The Barone's health was not good, and his son remembered him as 'old, pale and bent'. Giorgio would gaze 'with sadness and nostalgia at other boys whose fathers were still young and strong'. Doctors could not diagnose the illness which in 1905 turned out to be his last. His father knew that this would be the case and apparently realized, too late, that he had not shown enough affection to his son. Giorgio remembered a late-spring evening in Athens when they were walking along a street together. 'Between me and my father, in spite of the deep affection which linked us together, there was a certain aloofness, an apparent coldness or, rather, a kind of reserve which prevented those spontaneous effusions found among people of mediocre birth.' It was a memorable moment: 'We walked in silence and the shadows of evening came down over the city.' His father placed his arm round the boy's shoulder. 'I was upset and embarrassed by this unexpected gesture of affection', and then his father spoke to him: 'My life is ending, but yours is hardly beginning.' They walked on in silence, and the next day his father was ill. A few days later the sight of a 'black pall flying in the wind' was to seem a presage: his father was dead. This was May 1905.

After the visits of condolence, the two boys and their mother kept vigil over their father's body all night. After midnight Giorgio was the only one who remained awake. 'Then I tiptoed into my bedroom, took some paper and a pencil and returned to draw by candlelight my father's profile as he lay in the sleep of kindly death.' Deathbed portraits (and photography) were then quite usual, of course. 'My mother always kept this drawing and I believe my brother still has it.' That was written some forty years after his father's death, but surely the true commemoration of the death, and probably of the life too, was that enigmatic painting of 1914, *The Child's Brain*.

De Chirico was the first to acknowledge that the loss of his father affected him deeply – so deeply that he failed his final examination at the Athens Polytechnic, which took place two months later. It was surely bad luck that the subject he was asked to paint was 'an old man with a white beard who posed in the nude down to the waist, his head swathed in a turban, and his hand holding a long oriental pipe'. The figure in *The Child's Brain* was also 'nude down to the waist', and if the other details are irrelevant the coincidence is no less striking. The bereaved student did not believe he had been unfairly assessed by the examiners but decided that his 'failure was more or less justified', caused largely by his 'emotional shock'. For the first time he now admitted to suffering from 'frequent intestinal troubles', while 'the sultry heat of the Athenian July had made me feel tired, melancholy and discouraged, which certainly affected my work'. These health problems were to trouble him for a long time.

2
Paraphrase on the Finding of a Glove

In 1905 childhood and adolescence suddenly ended. Gemma de Chirico, now widowed, obviously wanted to ensure that her two sons continued the education that had begun so well, and she seems to have sought advice. If she herself had no family who could have offered it, she apparently did not lack in-laws and friends who soon helped to decide the future. She was advised to take her sons to Munich, where they could both continue their studies, Giorgio in art and Andrea in music.

As Giorgio later wrote in his *Memoirs*, Munich was the cultural centre of Europe at the time, 'rather', he continued, 'as Paris is today' – that is, in 1945. To anyone living in Greece in the first decade of the twentieth century, Germany was not such a faraway foreign country as it might seem, for the country had been ruled by a German king, Otto of Bavaria, for thirty years, from 1832 to 1862. After he had been deposed by the military leaders of the time, his place had been taken by another ruler from northern Europe, Prince George of Denmark, who agreed to accept the throne from the Greek National Assembly. He ruled from 1863 until 1913, when he was assassinated.

The de Chirico family of three did not go to Germany immediately or directly, however. The house in Greece had to be sold, along with the furniture and many possessions, although the Baronessa did not sell her valuable Turkish carpets but kept them nearly all her life. Her husband's specialized library had to go, his books on 'mathematics, engineering and mechanics'. Then the plan was to go to Germany by way of Italy, which Gemma de Chirico may have seen with her husband in the past, although to her two sons it was unknown. Both men later wrote accounts of their journey, sometimes differing in the details. In the late summer they sailed from Patrasso in north-west Thessaly in a Greek ship, according to Giorgio, an Italian one according to Andrea, which was to take then directly to Venice. Giorgio was badly seasick and made a point of emphasizing that he was not the only sufferer: his brother was seasick too, although Andrea himself did not mention it.

Giorgio was so ill that he persuaded his mother to disembark at Bari and continue to Venice by rail. The only enjoyment that Giorgio found there were the ices and cream cakes at the Caffè Florian, but he could not get enough of them, for his mother seems to have insisted on endless visits to galleries, museums and churches. He developed a stiff neck through looking up at ceilings and high walls, concluding that, at seventeen, he was too young to appreciate the great painting of the past. He decided that it was the 'infinite stupidity' of adults that made them inflict this cultural tourism on their families.

When the family reached Milan, in September 1905, they visited the exhibition arranged as part of the celebrations to mark the opening of the Simplon tunnel under the Alps. Giorgio maintained that he saw and admired there the work of two modern Italian painters, Gaetano Previati and Giovanni Segantini, but the art critic and historian Maurizio Fagiolo dell'Arco believes that his memory failed him, for these two painters were not represented in this exhibition. De Chirico presumably saw them a few years later, when he stayed in Florence and was by then in a position to appreciate them. Previati, who was still alive at the time – he lived from 1852 to 1920 – usually painted historical subjects and landscapes but did not neglect symbolism and was regarded as one of the rare Italian representatives of art nouveau. De Chirico apparently preferred his work to that of Segantini, although the two Italian painters shared the same qualities: 'poetry and metaphysics'. (Some five years later de Chirico spelled out what he understood by 'the metaphysical aspect of things', having studied the German thinkers Schopenhauer and Nietzsche while in Munich. In his visionary essay 'On Metaphysical Art', probably written in Paris in 1915, but not published until 1919, he said, 'One can deduce and conclude that every object has two aspects: one current one which we see nearly always and which is seen by men in general, and the other which is spectral and metaphysical and seen only by rare individuals in moments of clairvoyance and metaphysical abstraction . . .') It was typical of the young painter that he praised the lesser known of the two, but Segantini, who lived from 1858 to 1899, had been more concerned with symbolism and had used a semi-impressionist or 'divisionist' technique that would not have appealed so much to de Chirico. He had concentrated on the rendering of light, studying it especially in the evening, and had become well known for his paintings of mountain landscapes in the Alps.

In his *Memoirs* de Chirico did not mention that the family stayed in Florence for a time, but his presence there was recorded by the Accademia di Belle Arti, where he seems to have followed a course for a year. It was probably at this time that he and his brother were able to visit their eccentric uncle Gustavo, who still lived in the city, in the via Ricasoli. Gustavo was apparently persuaded on at least one occasion to visit Giorgio's studio and was so upset by a painting he saw on the easel there that he fled in horror: it was too 'modern'. The year in Florence apparently convinced Giorgio that if he wanted to become a truly successful painter he needed to follow a more disciplined training, and if there had previously been any doubt about going to Munich it was now dispelled.

When he arrived in Germany Giorgio found he was not prepared for the atmosphere there: everything was so different from the background to his childhood in Greece, where the haunting vestiges of classical times contrasted with the violent changes of climate and the aggressive Turkish neighbours. He now enjoyed a tranquillity he had never known before: 'The pine forests, a few scents that were new to me, a certain type of order to which I was not accustomed, gave me a sense of well-being.' Everything was clean and well organized, there were no beggars, and the frothy beer came in 'tankards resembling small cathedrals' and was served by 'shapely, blonde and full-breasted waitresses'. The eighteen-year-old student decided at first that this was 'paradise on earth'.

By the time he was writing his *Memoirs* the former student had developed into a crusty, middle-aged man who spent page after page attacking 'modern art', which, he believed, had been caused partly at least by the painting of the Sezession – 'the dominating influence at that time'. This movement – so named because during the 1890s various groups of artists in Germany and Austria broke away or 'seceded' from the traditional academic styles – had arrived in Munich in 1892, reached Vienna in 1898 (headed for five years by Gustav Klimt) and appeared in Berlin in 1899 (led for ten years or so by Max Liebermann). The end of the nineteenth century did not mean the end of the 'decadents' and the symbolists among its members, and in 1906 they were still almost 'modern'. De Chirico surely visited all the museums and art galleries and would also presumably have seen the work of several painters whose influence on him has been noted – Anselm Feuerbach (1829–80), for instance, who painted mythological figures such as Antigone, Iphigenia and Circe. There was also Franz von Lenbach (1836–1904), a leading figure in Munich during the late nineteenth century, a portrait painter in the Venetian style who had learned his technique in Italy. He was famous for having painted no fewer than eighty portraits of the great Bismarck, the 'Iron Chancellor'. The student painter mentioned none of these artists by name in his *Memoirs*, however, but restricted himself to condemning the Sezession (in Munich at least) as 'one of the two events . . . excessively harmful for humanity . . . These two events were modern painting and Nazism.' De Chirico would also surely have seen work by Caspar David Friedrich (1774–1840), the quietly impressive painter of the romantic era whose work had been rediscovered by the symbolists. As in France, where all the great romantic writers also drew or painted, many of these German painters supplemented their work with memorable words, and one of Friedrich's sayings seems particularly relevant in the context of de Chirico's painting and his insistence on its 'metaphysical' content: 'Close your bodily eye,' wrote Friedrich, 'so that you see your picture first with your spiritual eye, then bring to the light of day that which you have seen in darkness so that it may react on others from the outside inwards.'

By far the most important influence on de Chirico during these intensely formative years received only a passing mention in this phase of the *Memoirs*, but his young admirer never forgot him and was to publish a serious study of him in 1920. This 'hero', this 'icon', was the Swiss-born Arnold Böcklin, who lived from 1827 to 1901, spending a good part of his life in Italy. Fiercely fighting centaurs, unattractive naiads, unidentifiable animals, heavy cliffs and ponderous rocks: all these typical Böcklin motifs have lost their appeal a hundred years after they were produced, but the painter cannot be entirely forgotten, for he is said to have influenced German expressionism and he painted, in more than one version, that classic of nostalgic mourning *The Island of the Dead*, with its tomb among the cypresses and its atmosphere of stillness and silence which seems more than a mere technical achievement. The painting had been commissioned by a young widow and was originally entitled *A Tranquil Place*. Its popularity was so enduring that both painter and painting were sanctified by the artist Ferdinand Keller in *The Tomb of Böcklin*. No doubt the tomb was built in imagination on that same island, now sentimentalized in this later painting by a veil of mauve wisteria. But de Chirico saw qualities much deeper than Böcklin's popular success: he did not not see the dreary, muddy painter who fails to attract admirers today; he saw 'a classic in the purest sense of the word'. Mysterious figures – often hooded or veiled – in enigmatic situations: it is the de Chirico scene before de Chirico. The younger painter was to set out in detail all the reasons for his admiration in 1920, but the biographer can see that de Chirico was impressed by the *Stimmung* he found in Böcklin's painting, that hard-to-translate German word which he liked to interpret as 'atmosphere in the moral sense'. De Chirico regarded Böcklin as 'classical in the purest sense of the word'; in his work there was 'always little composition and very little embellishment', and de Chirico was particularly impressed by 'the revelation of that inexplicable something that fills the creative artist with divine joy'.

De Chirico was quick to learn languages and to appreciate the *correspondances* (in the Baudelairean sense) between what was seen and felt and written. In Germany, Schopenhauer, the influential thinker, and Nietzsche, the philosopher-poet, were ever-present; indeed, Nietzsche had died only recently, in 1899. De Chirico was to invoke them in his writing all his life and by inference in his painting. A polychrome statue of Nietzsche was designed by the other German artist whom de Chirico greatly admired, Max Klinger, himself an admirer of Böcklin. Klinger's best-known work outside Germany now is the intriguing set of etchings, a kind of superior strip cartoon, entitled *Paraphrase on the Finding of a Glove*. It portrays the fantasy of sexual pursuit in an atmosphere half real, half unreal, its erotic overtones seeming to anticipate Freudian theory. Another work, *The Nightmare*, is reminiscent of William Blake or Fuseli, leading to the view that Klinger was a surrealist *avant la lettre*. That view would not have appealed to de Chirico, but in 1921 he wrote of Klinger, who had died the previous year, as 'the modern artist par excellence. Modern not in the sense currently given to that word, but in the sense of a man of awareness who feels the heritage of centuries and centuries of art and thought, who sees clearly into the past, into the present and into himself.' In his *Memoirs* de Chirico included Klinger in the list of artists he had understood by the time he was seventeen, but if he had seen Klinger's work by then it was surely the atmosphere of Germany that allowed him to understand it and relate it to the painting that was in his mind if not yet on canvas. He certainly never forgot Klinger's symbolic use of the glove.

If Klinger was perhaps sinister in some ways, the Austrian Alfred Kubin was most of the time infinitely depressing – especially as a writer – but his drawings of Italian squares (including at least one showing a large winged horse standing on a plinth) very probably had some influence on de Chirico.

Another Austrian made a great impression on the young de Chirico, if only for a time: Otto Weininger, who shot himself for a bet at the age of twenty-three in 1903, choosing Beethoven's house in Vienna for the deed. Two of his books became important to the younger man: *Sex and Character* of 1901 and especially the later *Concerning Supreme Things*, which has much to say about the symbolism of geometric shapes and talks of metaphysics in relation to painting. Like Klinger, Weininger was an admirer of Böcklin, but later in life de Chirico decided that Weininger did not interest him any more. One reason for this may have been that Weininger, like Schopenhauer and Nietzsche before him, took what now seems a limited view of women, to put it kindly, although it was no more than fairly typical of its time. Weininger believed that a woman had no soul, no imagination and therefore could never become a composer or an architect. In *Sex and Society* he went further: 'Where, however, a weak and vague sentimentality can be expressed with little effort, as in painting or verse-making, or in pseudo-mysticism and theosophy, women have sought and found a suitable field for their efforts.' He also pointed out that men had established an ideal woman, the Madonna, but women had 'made no ideal of man to correspond with the male conception of the Madonna. What woman requires from man is not purity, chastity, morality, but something else. Woman is incapable of desiring virtue in a man.' By 1945 or before, when de Chirico was writing his *Memoirs*, he had been inseparably married to his second wife for at least a decade and had presumably learned something about women. At the same time, as both de Chirico's wives were Jewish, he would have condemned Weininger's virulent anti-Semitism.

De Chirico had no good word for his fellow students in Munich: he found them incompetent and compared them unfavourably with those he had known in Athens, who had been 'full of talent and full of romantic temperament and love for painting'. One of his few friends was a manic-depressive who committed suicide. He did not mention a single teacher by name. Soon he found himself living 'a colourless and boring existence,' although there were a few diversions – playing billiards, walking in the countryside and climbing in the nearby Bavarian Alps. He did not refer to the many buildings in Munich which must surely have made some impression on him, nor to the many art galleries and museums. He did, however, mention that he was at that time 'a great Wagnerian' and never missed a chance to listen to Wagner's music. Later he recanted: 'Today I have lost my love for that music in which I feel something mawkish and immoral, something which is also perhaps bad.' In 1945, when this was written, de Chirico was at least politically correct, given Hitler's known love of Wagner, and may have forgotten the composer's great hope – unfulfilled – that Böcklin would design scenery for his operas. Böcklin, apparently, did not approve of Wagner, although Weininger did.

By 1909 Giorgio had travelled back to Milan with his mother and brother. Andrea had hoped that the successful composer Pietro Mascagni, whom he had met in Munich, would help him to arrange the performance of an opera he had composed, but the famous Italian soon lost interest and Andrea was disappointed. At one point the music publishing house Ricordi seemed about to publish the opera, *Carmela*, but dropped the idea and the work was subsequently lost. It seems likely that these early experiences eventually influenced Andrea when he decided, some six or seven years later, to give up composition for many years, but for the time being he continued to compose and to write libretti. His elder brother noted that he also 'drew and painted'.

The brothers were far from idle: they both 'read and studied a good deal', and they also worked with a teacher of Latin. However, the little family group seemed to be drifting. They had all been disappointed by Andrea's failures, while Giorgio experienced failure too: he attempted to arrange a small exhibition of his recent paintings but without success.

Since there seemed no point in staying any longer in Milan, the trio decided to go to Florence, although Giorgio remembered that there was 'no particular reason' for the change. All his life he hated moving. As things turned out, the move to Florence was crucial in this chrysalis year of 1910. The city and its buildings were now to influence him deeply, and he knew that Böcklin had lived near by for a long time. While in Milan he had painted 'canvases of a Böcklinesque flavour' which only art historians and specialists would recognize as his. Some of them are almost indistinguishable from those of the older master, peopled as they are by centaurs – some frenzied, some dead – sirens, unenthusiastic musicians or Argonauts, seen sometimes against a would-be romantic landscape that might be rocky, tree-clad or maritime.

De Chirico made no secret of his bad health during 1909 and 1910. He was suffering surely from a depressive illness– apparently psychosomatic, for nothing seemed to cure it – a recurrence of the emotional problems experienced after his father's death and the mental turmoil, still unresolved, caused by the impact of his artistic and philosophical discoveries, especially Schopenhauer and Nietzsche, in Germany. He was attempting to 'paraphrase' them, to express in his painting the new insights he had received. He wrote that by the time he reached Florence the 'Böcklin period had passed', but he had introduced, even copied, into his paintings those enigmatic shrouded figures who seemed part of the mythological world he had seen in Böcklin and remembered imaginatively from the Greece of his childhood.

During the worst of his illness he had spent more time reading than painting, but he was beginning to emerge from the chrysalis. In his *Memoirs* he described in a few brief words what he was now trying to do: 'I had begun to paint subjects in which I tried to express the strong and mysterious feeling I had discovered in the books of Nietzsche.' But earlier, between 1911 and 1915, in some emotional notes formerly preserved in the collection of the poet Paul Eluard, he had written about this period in more detail. He referred to a trip he had made to Rome after his time in Munich, when he felt for the second time that he had not yet found his true direction. After reading Nietzsche, 'I became aware that there is a host of strange, unknown, solitary things which can be translated into painting. After much meditation I began to have my first revelations. I drew less, I even forgot how to draw . . .' He began to understand 'certain vague sensations', previously incomprehensible: 'The language that the things of this world sometimes speak; the seasons of the year and the hours of the day. The epochs of history too: prehistory, and the revolutions in thought throughout the ages, modern times . . .' It is a fascinating piece, essential reading for anyone wishing to understand how 'metaphysical' painting came into being, although it provides no easy explanation: 'One must picture everything in the world as an enigma.'

In his *Memoirs* de Chirico set out another paraphrase: he had tried to paint 'the melancholy of beautiful autumn days, afternoons in Italian cities. It was the prelude to the squares of Italy painted a little later in Paris and then in Milan, in Florence and in Rome.' It is the painting of 1910 entitled *The Enigma of an Autumn Afternoon* that expresses most clearly what was going on in de Chirico's mind at the time: in front of a highly simplified version of the cathedral of Santa Croce the statue of Dante has been transformed into what looks like a typical Böcklin figure from ancient mythology, while in the distance hovers the sail of some ship beleaguered in this half-urban landscape. In one sense there was no 'enigma' about the ship – it was a memory of childhood and his visits to the harbour of Piraeus.

For part of this period in Florence de Chirico was alone. His health had grown worse for a time, and when his brother, accompanied by his mother, had returned to Munich for a performance of some of his music, Giorgio had felt too ill to make the journey.

While in Munich Andrea heard about the 'so-called "artistic revolution"' that was taking place in Paris. It was an exciting time: Picasso had already painted *Les Demoiselles d'Avignon*, Marinetti and his friends had published the futurist manifesto, the appearance of Diaghilev's Ballets Russes had revolutionized the theatrical world, and Apollinaire, who was later to play an important part in the careers of both brothers, had published his first book, *L'Enchanteur pourrissant*, in 1909. Andrea could not resist the rumours of this exciting atmosphere: he decided to go to Paris directly, on his own, while his mother returned to Florence, to her other son, ailing yet reading a good deal of philosophy and beginning to paint more meaningful canvases.

Before Andrea had left for Germany, Giorgio had found time and energy to paint his portrait in what Maurizio Fagiolo dell'Arco has called a 'Hamlet-like' pose. He wears a dark tunic with a lace collar; he stands as though framed by a glassless window, beyond which can be seen a hilly landscape and, almost like a coded signature, a centaur – a reminder that Böcklin had lived, worked and died very near Florence, while Andrea himself, when he began to draw, had introduced the typical Böcklinesque shrouded figure into at least one of his productions. If Giorgio thought he had 'forgotten how to draw', he had remembered by the time he painted this portrait.

The brothers were very close at this period of their lives: so close that when Andrea later wrote good news of Paris – 'a city full of life, movement, intelligent people and that it would be even in my interest to go there' – Giorgio, although he disliked travelling, gave in to his brother's persuasive suggestion that the family should join him. He would go to Paris.

The two years in Germany had complemented his studies in Greece and he had discovered the German thinkers – reversing past trends when German writers, painters and thinkers had discovered Italy. His health if anything was worse, and there is no evidence to show whether his mother approved of this move to Paris or not. In 1911 Giorgio was twenty-three, but his mother surely felt that he needed her still. Soon he needed her as a model, and the portraits he painted of the two of them together express the whole story of their relationship. When writing about her in his *Memoirs* he remained factual, whereas he told something of his emotional relationship with his father. If women entered his inner world, he said nothing about them, and when he mentioned the death of his elder sister, Adèle, when he was about two or three he concentrated on the fact that the nursemaid appointed to see that he avoided the sight of the funeral cortège failed to obey her orders. It was surely her early bereavement that made the Baronessa so deeply protective of her two sons, as later observers did not fail to notice her to be.

At the same time the human figures in Giorgio's painting, living or sculptured, were usually sexless, sometimes faintly masculine but never feminine.

3
'A City Full of Life, Movement, Intelligent People'

IT sounded exhilarating, tempting, and the extrovert Andrea was obviously enjoying himself. Giorgio, however, still struggling to organize the ideas he had brought back from Germany and developed further since his return to Italy, wondering how he could translate them into painting, struggling too with his health problems – at least partly psychosomatic in origin – did not seem impatient to leave Florence. Through its buildings, light and atmosphere that ancient and beautiful city seemed to express the concepts, poetic and philosophical, that he had been reading about in Schopenhauer and Nietzsche. He surely regretted leaving it, aware that he was still a long way from achieving his ambitions as a painter. In many ways he was exhausted, and, although he had agreed to go to Paris, he probably dreaded the idea of yet another move, yet another journey.

It is not known whether he persuaded his mother to stop at Turin on the way or whether it was her idea, but the route through Piedmont probably appealed to him more than a possible sea voyage to Marseilles. Since leaving Greece he had seen Venice, he had visited Rome, and the family of three had stayed in Milan and Florence for a year or so in each city. They had therefore seen the most famous of the larger cities in the north of the country. Giorgio would certainly have known that Nietzsche, whom he still read constantly, had spent happy and creative months in Turin before his mental collapse there in 1889.

Turin, the capital of Piedmont, was and is a unique city, with a rich if disturbed history. In 1861 the first Italian parliament met there and proclaimed the King of Piedmont to be the first King of Italy, Vittorio

Emmanuele II. Three years later the architect Alessandro Antonielli began to build the famous Mole Antonelliana, the vast structure which has remained a focal point in the city. Strangely, perhaps, the building was intended to be a synagogue when it was started in 1863; it was completed thirty-four years later by the civic authority, reaching a height of eighty-six metres. In 1953, after it had lost nearly half its height in a damaging storm, it was repaired with aluminium. Did de Chirico remember the Mole when he included impossibly tall structures in some of his later paintings? Perhaps. But what he remembered most clearly from Turin were the long arcades, the wide piazzas and the statues. These latter included an impressive equestrian statue by Carlo Marochetti commemorating a victorious military leader; but perhaps more important were the statues of famous citizens, notably Giovanni Batista Bottero, a frock-coated philosopher. These figures were erected on low plinths, not high pedestals, and there was a particular reason for de Chirico to admire them: his hero Schopenhauer, who had written memorably about statues, had made a point of praising this system, not limited to Turin, for the way it made passers-by feel closer to the people commemorated, as if the 'men of marble' were almost on their level, almost alive.

The painter and his mother apparently stayed only two days in Turin, in July 1911, and saw an exhibition which had just opened. The *Memoirs* include no details of what was on show, but this visit was to be important to de Chirico very soon, for it left him with a kind of short-term nostalgia; it became a key element in that mixture of mystery, melancholy and enigma. He does not seem to have thought of prolonging the stay in Turin, but during the journey on to Paris he reacted as he had done during the journey from Greece to Venice a few years earlier. It was summer and very hot; he soon felt ill. He urged his mother to break the journey across France; she was worried and agreed to do so. They left the train at Dijon, less than 200 miles from Paris, and went to a hotel. Giorgio was seen by a doctor who prescribed hot poultices on his stomach, which meant that his mother spent most of the night in and out of the hotel kitchens boiling water.

After he had been administered a laudanum-based sedative, her son eventually slept for a long time and felt well enough t Paris train that evening. 'We reached the Gare de Lyon in of the night. My brother was waiting for us. When he saw tell from his expression that I must have looked in very bad shape.' On account of their stays in Turin and Dijon, Giorgio and his mother had probably forgotten the date, or, as the Baronessa may never have been in France before, they perhaps had not realized its significance: 'It was the night of July 14th and Paris was celebrating: people were dancing on the pavements in front of the cafés where barrel-organs and orchestras were playing non-stop.'

Giorgio did not find the peace and quiet he needed for some time, for there were more temporary stays: first in a hotel, then in a pension, then in an apartment which his mother furnished 'as best she could' in the rue de Chaillot, in the sixteenth arrondissement between the Etoile and the Seine. A little later a doctor advised the ailing Giorgio to take a cure at Vichy, where difficult cases have been and still are treated, sometimes with near-miraculous results. The treatment seemed to work, and the patient came back to Paris convinced that he was completely well. He remembered two facts: Julius Caesar had been cured of dyspepsia by the *aquae calidae* of Vichy, and his own father had gone there for convalescence after a bout of malaria. Giorgio did no painting for some time, but his long rest was helpful in the end: 'I took up again the thread of inspiration which I drew from Nietzsche.'

In the meantime he had to catch up with the activities of his energetic brother, who had immersed himself in all the varied excitement of the Paris scene. Andrea, arriving in 1910, had found a city, a country in fact, which had moved on from the *belle époque* into a very different era. Within one year, 1905, the French Socialist Party had come into existence and the Catholic Church had formally separated from the state. Among the rare good news of the early century had been the pardon finally granted to Alfred Dreyfus in 1906. But three years later the sinister right-wing organization *L'Action française* began to publish a newspaper. Strikes by workers and the terrorism of the infamous *bande à Bonnot* have led some historians to think that during this period the power and prestige of France began to decline. Nobody realized how soon the so-called 'banquet years' would come to an end.

Meanwhile there was indeed plenty of 'movement', as Andrea had found – fresh developments in science and technology and endless novelty in all the arts. In music, theatre, painting and writing new trends were coexisting with the old ones – Debussy's *Pelléas and Mélisande* (1902), Maeterlinck's *Blue Bird* (1908), the Ballets Russes of Diaghilev (from 1909), all the 'isms' that followed impressionism, Marinetti's *Manifesto of Futurism* (launched in Paris in 1909) – yet the old-style writers such as Anatole France continued to be published and read. The Fauves held a big exhibition in 1905 (the year after Apollinaire probably met Picasso), and two years later the cubists followed their example. The cubist movement, led by Picasso and Braque, was now in its 'analytical' phase, in which forms, like society, seemed to have been fractured. Alfred Jarry, creator of *Ubu Roi* (1896), had died of alcoholism in 1907, while the strange, endearing and influential Douanier Rousseau followed him in 1910. The English novelist Arnold Bennett, who was living in Paris at the time, was less interested in painters than in writers, but he visited the celebrated Durand-Ruel Galleries, which dealt in Renoir and his contemporaries, where he noted that there was no doubt about the potential buyers: 'Certainly the chief languages spoken were American and Japanese.' Bennett recorded no reaction to the rumours that de Chirico heard soon after his arrival, talk of 'revolutionary painters, Picasso and Cubism, the modern schools . . .'

Nothing was too modern for Andrea, who was now beginning to call himself Alberto Savinio, adapting the name from that of a 'polygraph' called Albert Savine, now unremembered. He was already earning a reputation for himself, at least among friends, partly through his eccentric piano recitals (of which more later) and partly through his enthusiastic but still unperformed operatic compositions.

Andrea and Giorgio were known for a time as the 'Dioscuri', a term they had used when they much younger in Greece, reminding themselves and all who knew them of those famous twin sons of Zeus. People who met them assumed that they influenced each other, although they were working in different fields. Andrea had already met Picasso, Cocteau, Apollinaire – the latter two, especially Apollinaire, were to be important to both brothers later – while through his main preoccupation, music, he had also met the Franco-Greek musicologist Michel-Dmitri Calvocoressi, and the two had begun to work together on an opera with a mysterious title, *Le Trésor de Rampsenit*, but it was never completed. Calvocoressi knew painters as well as musicians, and when he met Giorgio he advised him to submit some work to the 1912 Salon d'Automne. Calvocoressi suggested he should visit his acquaintance Pierre Laprade, a successful painter at the time, now forgotten, who was a member of the Salon jury.

It is impossible to improve on the young painter's later description of what was to be the starting point of his career. The night before his visit, de Chirico had a dream in which he saw 'a landscape somewhat similar to the banks of the lakes in Lombardy and the Lake Garda region. In the foreground were a few trees and some pink blossom; in the background was a stretch of water like a mirror.' Then he had a surprise: 'When I entered Laprade's studio the next day I saw . . . standing on an easel, a painting that represented a landscape identical with the one I had seen in my dream.' When he told Laprade about his dream, the older man 'smiled and said, "*Tiens, c'est rigolo.*"' He also added that he often painted in the Lombardy region. De Chirico's comment on this – made, of course, long after the event – was in the style that had become typical of him: 'From which I deduced that the painter Pierre Laprade did not show the same interest in the metaphysics and mystery of dreams as someone like Pythagoras or Arthur Schopenhauer.' However, Laprade proved as useful as Calvocoressi had hoped: he advised the young man to submit three paintings, 'not too big', and said he would make sure that the jury accepted them.

The jury did so, accepting all three, which consisted of a self-portrait and two others which included that characteristic word in their titles: *The Enigma of the Oracle* and *The Enigma of an Autumn Afternoon.* They were well hung, said the painter, in a room reserved for foreign artists, were favourably mentioned by a few critics but were not sold. The painter himself was listed in the catalogue as 'Georgio [*sic*] de Chirico, born in Florence', his address in Paris being given as 43 rue de Chaillot.

In one sense he *had* been 'born in Florence', although he had painted very little there (and less still since his arrival in Paris), but the two 'enigma' paintings – and even the self-portrait carried the question 'What shall I love if not the enigma?' – marked the true beginning of the metaphysical style. The 'enigma' lay in the mysterious relationship between the real and the unreal. 'Every profound work of art', he wrote later in his important 1919 piece 'On Metaphysical Art', 'contains two solitudes.' There was the 'plastic solitude', but 'Only in the new Italian metaphysical painting does the second solitude appear: solitude of signs, or the metaphysical.' (By the time he wrote and published this piece, de Chirico had in fact almost come to the end of his 'metaphysical' period.) He would know better than many other painters and critics that the word 'enigma' was derived ultimately from the Greek words *ainissesthai*, to speak darkly, and *ainos*, a fable. He was telling the story of his own mysterious discoveries, the 'surprise' that his mentor Nietzsche had extolled. 'When Nietzsche talks of how Zarathustra was conceived and says: "I was surprised by Zarathustra", in this participle – surprised, is contained the whole enigma of sudden revelation.' This sentence, from the manuscript formerly in the Paul Eluard collection, written between 1911 and 1915, is another of many similar references to Nietzsche in de Chirico's prose fragments of this period and his later articles.

De Chirico had not been influenced by all the experimental work going on around him in Paris at the time: once the influence of Böcklin had faded, he showed himself to be his own man, and at this stage nothing would deflect him from the philosophical ideas with which he appeared obsessed. Critics were apparently interested by the individuality of his work, but it was too early for a positive reaction from buyers. They were hardly likely to respond to those cryptic titles: they were interested in prices, not in philosophical works they had never read.

It would be a mistake all the same to assume that de Chirico was the only man outside Germany who had reacted to the ideas that lay behind his early work. There was the Italian Giovanni Papini, for instance, a Florentine who, in addition to his writing, editing and acerbic reviewing, had translated Schopenhauer into Italian and absorbed much of his thought. De Chirico and Papini were friends for years, but later, in 1919, they quarrelled bitterly, and in his *Memoirs* de Chirico makes two disparaging mentions of Papini. Papini was as argumentative as de Chirico was to be, while he was also eccentric, destructive and unpredictable. Another possible influence was Dino Campana, sometimes called 'the Italian Rimbaud', although his *Canti orfici* had not been published in 1914, while the well-known if very different Gabriele d'Annunzio showed that de Chirico could not claim to be the only person preoccupied with metaphysical thought and the images that expressed it. To quote one critic, Maurizio Calvesi, d'Annunzio's work included themes touching on 'infinity, solitude, mystery and enigma, deserted streets, silent piazzas overshadowed by equestrian monuments, the statue embodying suspense and waiting, towers, foreboding' and even the lonely figure in a black robe 'gazing thoughtfully at the horizon'. De Chirico, however, was the only painter in France at the time who attempted to incorporate such images, such near-abstractions, such preoccupation with the real and the unreal into his work. He was in no way tempted by all the 'modernistic' developments round about him; he was not to be deflected from the solitary course he had chosen – one that seemed almost an obsession.

By 1912 the 'banquet years' were coming to an end, although the international crowd of painters in Paris hardly noticed events outside their studios, a few galleries and exhibitions. The futurists were active in France and Italy, responding in their way to new scientific discoveries and the growing cult of speed. In 1912 their leader, Marinetti, published his *Technical Manifesto of Futurist Literature*, while the sculptor and painter Umberto Boccioni brought out a similar work about sculpture. The latter's paintings interpret speed in such a striking way that his wartime death in 1916 is all the more regrettable, but at least he escaped the group's later wretched political decline into Fascism. May 1913 brought the première of the Stravinsky–Nijinsky ballet *The Rite of Spring*; Alberto Savinio, as he can now be called, attended this performance and vowed that he would dedicate himself to ballet music. In literature, Marcel Proust was completing the first part of his great work which was to be published the following year. The poet Paul Valéry, whose intellectual rigour and rejection of symbolist excesses were to have a formative influence on André Breton, the future leader of the surrealists, was to remain silent until 1917, but these years also saw the publication of two works even more influential on future writing and painting: Jung's *Psychology of the Unconscious* and Freud's *Totem and Taboo*. While Freud and Jung were exploring the unconscious, the man who was to study its role in the creative process and bring writing and painting close together, Breton himself, was a schoolboy of sixteen or so at the Collège Chaptal. He was writing his own early poetry and was about to make an important discovery: in the Gustave Moreau museum in the rue La Rochefoucauld in Montmartre he saw the exotic work of that leading symbolist painter who had taught two such different artists as Rouault and Matisse. Under Moreau's influence Breton now began to perceive and understand the mysteries of love and sex, dominated by Woman as the powerful symbol of eroticism.

These mysteries were to become crucial in the surrealist code (not, of course, formulated yet). But how did de Chirico see them? He was fond of using the word 'mystery', but he had probably not forgotten the prudish atmosphere of his childhood, and, after all, he still lived with his mother. He certainly did not include women in his early painting. Although his Böcklin-style productions include a flabby and unattractive nereid with breasts like those of the waitresses in Munich, other works include figures whose robes seem to cover a body that is sexless. The mysterious seer-like figures, whose faces are usually turned away, seem conveniently hermaphrodite, while if a woman is included, as in *Melancholia* of 1912 or 1913, she is Ariadne (who was deserted by Theseus) and is no human but a reclining statue, shown in a pose said to be based on the famous and beautiful Ariadne in the Vatican Museum, a Roman work copied from the Greek. De Chirico in fact modelled a small sculptured Ariadne figure in a similar pose during the same year, and used the Ariadne theme (often mentioned by

Nietzsche) in several paintings, some with her name in the title, some without.

Although real women did not yet exist in his paintings, they had begun to exist in his life, even if there was no emotional relationship to speak of. The most important one was still his mother, perpetually there as she and her two sons moved first to the rue Campagne-Première in the fourteenth arrondissement and then to the rue Notre-Dame-des-Champs, in the sixth. During the 1970s de Chirico's first wife, Raissa, told the writer Luisa Spagnoli that in 1914 or so, in the house opposite that occupied by de Chirico ménage, there lived 'a very beautiful girl, a kind of prostitute, and that Giorgio, who was twenty-five or twenty-six at the time, had developed a great crush on her'. This girl had many clients but, like most prostitutes, she needed an *amant de coeur*, who did not have to pay for her sexual favours. She had chosen Giorgio. This was just as well, for he was frustrated by lack of money. Presumably he was able to buy the materials he needed for his painting, but these costs were not covered by his sales. Since he and his brother were due to inherit funds from the estate of their late father, he decided to ask his mother for an advance. But the Baronessa refused to give him any money, possibly assuming that he might waste it buying gifts for the beautiful girl, and she continued to dominate her elder son. However, he took action, moving out of the family apartment and joining the girl in the house across the road, so inflicting a minor defeat on this controlling parent. He was presumably happy, if poverty-stricken, while 'his mother, looking through her windows, could see her son leaning against the balcony of the house opposite, observing the passers-by for hours'.

Most other parents would have expected some rebellion; it was said that the Baronessa expected her two sons to dress respectably for dinner even when the meal was taken at home. They were also expected to accompany her on outings such as shopping expeditions, for which she herself dressed well and wore the jewellery to which she was so attached.

He was, however, more outgoing about his work: he had realized that there could be no success without the right personal contact. 'I sought out Guillaume Apollinaire,' he wrote, and this was the starting point for the work that was to make him famous. Savinio already knew Apollinaire, for every young painter, writer or musician had heard of him and wanted to know him. Few men of the early twentieth century were more creative, more perceptive, more unlucky – especially in love and, as it turned out, in war. Everything had been against him or at least seemed to be so. Born in Rome in 1880, he was the illegitimate son of Angela de Kostrowitzky, the daughter of a chamberlain to the Pope. His father may have been Francesco Flugi d'Aspremont, an Italian, but the son himself had no citizenship and, despite some lycée education, no qualifications – and no money. However, his intelligence and charm took him eventually, by way of ghost-writing, clandestine erotic works and minor journalism, into the literary and artistic world that was his natural habitat. In 1908, some ten years after his arrival in Paris, André Gide met him at a literary banquet: 'Very much amused and attracted by Apollinaire's face,' he wrote, and a little later the Douanier Rousseau included that face and figure (which were both large) in his painting *The Muse Inspiring the Poet*, shown at the Salon des Indépendants in 1909. Apollinaire's bad luck included losing the manuscript of a novel on a train, brief imprisonment after being falsely accused of stealing the Mona Lisa and other exhibits from the Louvre and several rejections as a lover, first by an English girl and then by the young painter Marie Laurencin, who was beginning to make a name for herself but did not wish to be Apollinaire's muse. His novel *L'Hérésiarque et cie* did well in the first round of voting for the 1910 Goncourt Prize, and two years later, with three friends, he founded the review *Les Soirées de Paris*, writing the lead essay, 'Du sujet dans la peinture moderne', and concluding that in the end the subject of a painting did not really matter. By the end of the year he had taken over the review and moved to the address that he made famous: the top floor of 202 *bis* boulevard Saint-Germain.

Les Soirées de Paris, which continued until the outbreak of war, included several pieces of work by Savinio but only brief mentions of his elder brother's painting. However, Picasso had noticed his work, and even thought he had 'discovered' him, mentioning him to

Apollinaire, who was in no way put off by Picasso's alleged remark that the young Italian was 'the painter of railway stations'. (Savinio believed that paintings such as *The Enigma of the Hour* (1912), with its clock at five to three, and others with a similar architectural background were based on the Gare Montparnasse, not far from Giorgio's studio at 115 rue Notre-Dame-des-Champs.)

Apollinaire had advised his young friend to send work to the 1913 Salon des Indépendants, and he did so. De Chirico recalled what happened in the same mood in which he had described his visit to Pierre Laprade before the Salon d'Automne in 1912. He complained about the attitude of two members of the selection committee, André Dunoyer de Segonzac and Luc-Albert Moreau: they described his paintings as very 'decorative' and told him that he would make a good stage designer. According to the painter, thinking back thirty years later, this showed 'that they had in no way understood the exceedingly solitary and profound lyricism of these paintings'. They were not alone, however, for he believed (in 1945) that nobody had ever understood them, and he went on to attack the surrealists, 'the leaders of modernistic imbecility'. However, within ten years or so de Chirico was invited to make his first stage designs, and he continued this aspect of his work until the end of his life.

He also recorded in his offhand style his memories of Apollinaire's Saturdays: 'Painters, poets and literati came, the so-called "young" and "intelligent" people who put forward the so-called "new ideas".' He mentioned the 'taciturn and thoughtful individuals' who sat around smoking clay pipes. 'On the walls were pictures by Marie Laurencin, Picasso and a few obscure cubists whose names I have forgotten. Later two or three of my metaphysical paintings were also hung there . . .' In *Casa 'La Vita'* Savinio described Marie Laurencin as wearing 'a little postilion's hat with a little black spotted veil . . . and a bunch of artificial violets pinned to her muff'. He also found that her voice reminded him of melodies from some old-fashioned operetta, like Boïeldieu's *The White Lady*. His elder brother, however, was quick to indicate why he himself went to these Saturday gatherings: 'I did so because I was still very young and therefore still fairly naïve and there were still many things I did not understand.' He hastened to add that he did not think much of his fellow guests: 'I did not have much esteem and sympathy for that ambiance and I was sometimes slightly bored there.' Maybe too he bored the others, by remaining aloof; he received some interest and cordiality, but the others were 'diffident towards me and detected in me an individual who was fairly different from them'.

He *was* different. His brother, who had helped him with introductions and watched his development, emphasized this in 1919, writing in the Italian magazine *Valori Plastici*. He reminded his readers that de Chirico

> lived for the most part outside the major artistic circles, [and] did not have occasion to be swept away . . . by the mechanism of formal evolution.
>
> One could say that, right from the beginning, he was concerned with spiritual affirmation. Nevertheless, since I was present during his time in Paris, I can state that he too, at this time, felt obliged to work through the course of the formal transformation of painting for his own benefit, and through all this to return again to a spiritual aim, which he was then able to affirm with complete organic plasticity.

In fact the years 1912, 1913 and 1914 saw de Chirico filling his canvases with all the images and memories that had crowded into his mind and demanded expression. The word 'melancholy' still appeared in several titles, but as his Böcklin-style figures receded or finally disappeared there was a new preoccupation with the 'infinite'. Towers appeared, immensely high, dwarfing the tiny figures seen on the ground. The one tower that seemed partly realistic was the famous *Rose Tower* of 1913, the very first painting that de Chirico sold, at that year's Salon des Indépendants, making him feel 'very pleased and proud'. However, in retrospect he could not refrain from the acrid comment that the buyer clearly didn't understand what the painting was about.

Who did? His brother, no doubt, for they had shared the same background, and very possibly Apollinaire, who, it has been said, had suggested some of the more colourful titles to the artist. Whatever the truth of that rumour, Apollinaire took him seriously. Just before the Salon des Indépendants he had been to the painter's studio to see thirty or so works that de Chirico had decided to show – practically all he had completed so far. The poet-critic did not care for the predominantly dark tones of the paintings but drew attention to the 'enigma' that deserved to be thought about. 'The art of this young painter', he wrote, 'is an interior and cerebral art that has no connection with the art of the painters who have appeared during these last years.' De Chirico had not been influenced by contemporaries such as Picasso or by the impressionists. Apollinaire pointed out a true originality that was 'very pronounced and very modern' and usually expressed through architecture.

Later, André Breton was to stress the sexual overtones of those towers and arcades, which appears obvious in the post-Freudian world, but Breton was convinced that de Chirico remained unconscious about how he might have been revealing the intimate secrets of his emotional life, the secret awareness that it was virtually non-existent. At this stage of his life he painted no ideal woman, and the *Nude* of 1911–12, with her drooping breast, is so unattractive that even the stone Ariadnes look beautiful in comparison. For once he had forgotten his philosophical concerns and attempted some realism, but he nevertheless filled out his painting with the inevitable dark building and a square-cut arch.

Apollinaire, who was apparently not very impressed by the discoveries of psychoanalysis, continued to follow de Chirico's work and noticed how it was evolving. He mentioned that the artist was painting 'display signs' and painting them for both picture galleries and midwives. Perhaps he was referring to that sinister rubber glove (a memory of Klinger, surely) hanging beside the head of Venus in *The Song of Love* and later in other works. Surfaces and perspectives were beginning to lose their stability, and Apollinaire introduced a note of gentle criticism when he described de Chirico, then working in the rue Campagne-Première, as 'the enemy of trees', hinting that he had been upset by the appearance of trees in the place de Rennes; he had preferred statues. Was de Chirico again depressed when in 1913 he painted a different kind of *Self-Portrait*, with objects which anyone could link with sexuality if they chose: an egg which casts an elongated shadow, a rolled-up scroll of paper, two factory chimneys, and two detached plaster feet, the right foot to the left of the left. He was probably not depressed, merely confused. The following year brought the painting of *The Child's Brain* – as mentioned earlier, possibly an unconscious memory of his father – and also a portrait of Apollinaire.

During the years since his meeting with Apollinaire, de Chirico had not only painted, he had begun to write, as if to complement the messages he hoped to be expressing on canvas. The fragments that were preserved among the papers of Paul Eluard and Jean Paulhan and published by James Thrall Soby in 1955 reveal a young man writing with a kind of lyricism about his awareness of the 'enigma': which is the real world, which is not? How can we find out? How can dreams and revelation affect us? The tone of voice here is essentially young, questioning, searching, meditating on prehistory and on painting old and new. It is the voice of a poet, and soon in fact de Chirico was to publish both poems and descriptions of dreams. (The manuscripts of some of these were later owned by Picasso.)

There were of course rumours of war, although nobody appeared too concerned. However, thoughts and images of war did appear in de Chirico's painting or have at least been construed as such. *The Day of the Fête* shows a topsy-turvy world; *The Philosopher's Conquest* includes a cannon; titles seem to carry a new atmosphere: *The Sailors' Barracks* and *The General's Illness* both belong to 1914, as do the previous two. But that these anticipate war can only be speculation. There were many developments at this stage of de Chirico's life, and especially important was his introduction by Apollinaire to the dealer Paul Guillaume, who was now to act for him, with the result that life improved – although de Chirico later complained about the practices of dealers in general. He was still close to his brother, and their mother watched over both of them.

On 24 May 1914 Giorgio and the Baronessa, along with Picasso,

Max Jacob, Paul Guillaume, the Italian futurist Ardengo Soffici and many others, went to the offices of *Les Soirées de Paris* to hear Savinio's first public recital of his composition *Musica sincerista*. The young musician described in one of his later stories this ground-floor apartment in the boulevard Raspail, its grey carpet, coloured rugs and furniture that had seen better days. There was a baby grand piano, which suffered, for Savinio tended to smash instruments with futurist destructiveness. Apollinaire, it was said, did not enjoy music, but he wrote enthusiastically about Savinio's style of playing. Sometimes the young pianist-composer stood up, he also took off his jacket but retained a monocle in his eye. Apollinaire described him as 'screaming and throwing himself about while his instrument struggles to attain his own pitch of enthusiasm'. Savinio was known to batter the keys so hard that his fingers bled and the blood had to be mopped up. The audience suffered the 'shock of the new' but soon came to recognize the 'profound originality' shown by the young man who called himself *un artisan dionysiaque*. The Paris intellectuals close to Apollinaire came to agree on one thing: this music and Giorgio's painting had an affinity – they were made up of memories and dreams and had virtually no links with any current trends.

Savinio wrote about his music in *Les Soirées de Paris*; he wanted, he said, to unite drama and music and most of all 'to reveal what modern metaphysics contains of drama, terrible, unknown and impassioned'. Drama: there was much of it in Savinio's work, although as time went on this became somewhat calmer; nevertheless, one is inevitably reminded of the one person in the family who may have been involved with the stage in the distant past – his mother. Possibly both her sons had inherited a sense of the theatre, never talked about in the family earlier but now expressing itself in different ways in the work of both Giorgio and Andrea/Alberto.

It was on 14 July 1913, two years to the day since he had come to Paris as an ailing and unknown young man, that de Chirico's work received its first favourable mention in Italy. It came unexpectedly from Ardengo Soffici, who was editor of the futurist periodical *Lacerba*. He had been impressed by Savinio's music and took the opportunity to add a perceptive passage about his brother's painting, stressing what several others had begun to say: it was unlike the work of anyone else, and it was not painting in the usual sense of the term: 'It could be described as the handwriting of dream.' He mentioned the fifteenth-century artist Paolo Uccello, not because he wanted to compare the art of the two painters but because they both painted with 'calm and application', they were 'in love with divine perspective and untouched by anything that did not possess its beautiful geometry'.

The calm and stillness in many, if not all, of de Chirico's works is all the more remarkable when one learns that Apollinaire, who knew him well, told André Breton that the painter often worked while suffering from the intestinal disorders that had plagued him earlier. If this was true, then he escaped the trauma of chronic psychosomatic illness by transforming it into the unsolvable enigma: the melancholy and mystery that in some magical fashion linked reality and dream.

In 1914, however, reality was to take over, if temporarily.

4
The Enigma of Fatality

'BUT the fatal year of 1914 arrived; it was summer, hot and sultry.' The conflict that in many ways marked the real end of the nineteenth century and changed the life of Europe for ever began in a start–stop manner. De Chirico remembered how 'everything became confused and uncertain', how, after the mobilization order on 1 August his small family group realized that the 'Germans were advancing on the capital'. But the de Chiricos still remained there for a few days, until Giorgio encountered the danger at first hand – a small bomb fell, causing at least two casualties, and he saw 'blood on the pavement'. As a result, 'my mother, brother and I went straight to a little seaside place in Normandy called Ouistreham'. Paul Guillaume, the dealer, went with them.

They were not refugees for long, and de Chirico – whose health seemed to have improved and given him an appetite – later made a point of remembering 'certain roast duck that were real poems'. During the Second World War too, until the Second Front operations late in the war involved Ouistreham at the eastern extreme of the sector chosen for the Allied landing, Parisians went to Normandy in order to eat well during the years of occupation. However, in 1914 the refugees were brought back to reality by the sight of wounded soldiers.

After the first battle of the Marne, won by a taxi-borne army during the week of 5–11 September, everyone assumed that Paris was no longer in danger, and the de Chirico family returned to find that 'the cafés were full of people and the boîtes in Montparnasse were functioning normally'. Two writers, Charles Péguy and Alain-Fournier, the latter the author of *Le Grand Meaulnes*, had been killed before the end of the month, but even this kind of news seems not to have upset literary and artistic circles for long.

However, life was far from normal for a great number of people, and many had left the capital. Some just wanted to escape; some did not know what to do. Apollinaire, who was not French and therefore not subject to mobilization, went to Cannes, where he had spent some time as a schoolboy and still had friends. He immediately fell in love (with Louise de Coligny-Châtillon), but when he was once again rejected he left for Nîmes and volunteered to serve in an artillery regiment. The girl, who was apparently impressed by this gesture, joined him – but not for long. The stateless poet realized that he could now acquire French citizenship, for which he yearned. He was soon sent to the front, and when not writing to another girl, whom he had met on a train, he wrote poems; he even succeeded in printing twenty-five copies of a small collection entitled *Case d'Armons*, using the special ink needed for the primitive military copying equipment.

André Gide was one of the few people who had actually come into Paris during the summer, and he went to meet Cocteau at an 'English tea-room'. 'He was dressed', Gide noted in his journal, 'almost like a soldier' – Cocteau was no doubt wearing the famous 'uniform' designed by the couturier Paul Poiret for his trips to the front with the ambulance unit which the society hostess Misia Sert had assembled from fashionable people like herself (although fortunately including one trained nurse). Gide added that 'the fillip of present events has made him look healthier'. It was a strange summer and autumn, during which writers in particular seemed to be acting a part. Colette, for instance, was a night-nurse in Paris for a time, before her secret visits to the war front where her husband, Henri de Jouvenel, was serving. Picasso, as a foreigner, had no military obligations, but it dawned on him one night when he, Gertrude Stein and Alice B. Toklas were walking down the boulevard Raspail that painters – cubist painters in particular – had unconsciously made a contribution to the modern military world. The trio saw 'a big cannon, the first any of us had seen painted, that is camouflaged. Pablo stopped, he was spellbound . . . it is we that have created that, he said. And he was right, he had. From Cézanne through him they had come to that.' In Britain the vorticist painter Edward Wadsworth, who served in the Royal Naval Reserve, had actually devised 'dazzle' camouflage for ships.

In Paris, painters, including de Chirico, continued to paint, although many well-known French artists, including Derain and Braque, were away at the front, and Maurice Vlaminck was working in an army paint store at Le Havre. De Chirico painted a good deal in the winter of 1914–15, as the dates of his paintings show, but there were no important exhibitions. Dealers could hardly be active, but it is known that five of his paintings were dispatched to the USA, apparently destined for the Steiglitz Gallery in New York, although it is not known if they arrived or were exhibited. Some of the paintings for which he is now best known were already owned by collectors, including Diaghilev, the dancer/choreographer Léonide Massine and the American Singer sewing-machine heiress Princesse Edmond de Polignac. Apollinaire had acquired *The Great Tower* of 1913 in addition to a sketch for his portrait or perhaps the portrait itself. Some of de Chirico's work was to have been exhibited in Germany at the premises of the review *Der Sturm*, but the war meant that the show was cancelled.

In May 1915 Italy entered the war, and de Chirico, along with other Italians in Paris, no longer had to endure pointed questions, especially from the *chansonniers*, asking when their country was going to take up arms and support France. He remembered later how he and his brother reacted: 'Spurred on by the same impulse that had led Apollinaire to enlist in the French army, I and my brother left for Florence, where we reported for call-up in the military district where we were registered.'

What was to happen to his paintings? Most of those that had been completed were in the hands of Paul Guillaume, but some were abandoned in the painter's studio in the rue Campagne-Première. Apparently the poet Giuseppe Ungaretti took over the studio, and at de Chirico's request he asked the writer Jean Paulhan, who lived in the same apartment block in Montparnasse, to help the painter, who was short of money, by selling the work. He mentioned that possibly André Gide and some of the future surrealists, André Breton and Philippe Soupault, might be interested – Louis Aragon too. He told Paulhan that he would be rewarded, naturally, by the gift of a painting.

De Chirico would not see Paris again for eight years, but through Paul Guillaume, various friends and the literary periodicals which continued to appear at irregular intervals he probably heard most of the news that mattered to him. Apollinaire, who never stopped writing, had spent the early part of the war falling in love and even became temporarily engaged. June 1914 had seen the publication of his intriguing pre-surrealist work *Lettre-Océan*; while from 1913 he had been working on the fascinating *Calligrammes*, poems of peace and war (published in 1918), in which poems were virtually transformed into drawings by typography. This latter collection included the hermetic poem 'Océan de terre', dedicated to de Chirico, who had given the author a drawing intended for a frontispiece. In the end a portrait by Picasso had been used instead, but de Chirico did not complain, for he regarded Picasso as a friend, for was it not Picasso who had arranged for Apollinaire to visit his basement studio in the early days, leading to admiration from Apollinaire and the appointment of Guillaume as his agent? Later, in 1930, a de-luxe edition of the poems was published with lithographs by de Chirico.

The painter was hardly likely to enjoy his initiation into army life, and he never forgot the 'symphony of smells' that greeted him at the barracks near Florence: 'greasy mess-tins, unwashed feet, carbolic, creosote and burnt coffee'. He naturally complained, in his *Memoirs*, about the offhand treatment he received from the officers, who assigned him to the infantry, but he could not complain about his posting to the old city of Ferrara in Emilia, long ruled by the dukes of Este and associated with two famous poets of the past, Ariosto and Tasso.

De Chirico saw no military action during the war but spent over two years in Ferrara creating works that brought his career to its peak – at least for those who believe that this career ended in 1924, even though he continued to paint for another five decades.

First of all he and his brother – they had remained together and were both given clerical work – were lucky enough to escape life in barracks but not through finding girlfriends or helpful landladies. Unlike Apollinaire, de Chirico, as far as is known, had no deeply emotional love affairs at this time. In 1913 he had painted a striking portrait of one Madame Gartzen and had mentioned to Paul Guillaume a portrait of '*mon amie*' that he did not want to sell, but there is no proof that these two portraits were one and the same, and nothing seems to be known about the relationship of painter and sitter. (The Gartzen portrait was thought lost for a time but in fact is safely owned by a private collector.) The two soldiers had a much better plan than girlfriends or landladies: they were joined in Ferrara by the one woman who still supplied a secure background to their lives – the Baronessa. 'Our mother came to Ferrara and rented a small furnished apartment; we could sleep at home, change our linen, eat plain, good food and, in our free time, think a little about those aspects of art and thought which had always been the most important part of our lives.' It was a matter of living *en famille* and going to the office every day, a long way from the Western Front, where, despite several important battles, the trench warfare was not leading to much territorial advance by either side. Yet a change had taken place in the attitude of the French public, especially when the Nobel Prize for Literature had been awarded in 1915 to Romain Rolland, whose pacifist views had not been popular earlier. The following year saw the publication of a famous anti-war novel, *Le Feu* by Henri Barbusse, which won the Goncourt Prize for the year. The jingoism of 1914 was over.

The de Chirico brothers certainly thought a good deal about 'aspects of art', leading Andrea/Alberto to an unexpected conclusion: in 1915 he decided to 'distance himself from music' out of 'fear'. He did not want music to take him over; he had found that it caused depression, that it could 'stupefy' those who practised it. His brother Giorgio had rejected music before he left Paris, writing that 'Music cannot express the essence of sensation. One never knows what music is about . . .' In fact Alberto returned to music late in life, but he had already published critical and creative work in reviews such as *Les*

Soirées de Paris (some of his earlier writing, dramatic dialogues in which the personae were not 'real' in the normal sense, is thought to have influenced aspects of the work produced by his brother shortly before the war), and he now went on to do so in Italian periodicals, leading to the publication of his first book, *Hermaphrodito*, in 1918. He also hoped to paint.

In these near-ideal Ferrara conditions Giorgio's own paintings became richer, no less enigmatic, often decorative, but constantly thought-provoking and, as things turned out, influential. Before he left Paris his painting had intrigued the critics mainly through its arcades, piazzas, towers and perspectives, 'normal' or not. Apart from the few portraits, which seemed to belong to another sphere of life, the human figure, or at least the 'normal' figure, had been absent. The onlooker could have assumed that de Chirico was not interested in people or that he was frightened of them or despised them. He now began to introduce half-human figures, as though this were a step forward from the marble or plaster heads and reclining statues; he had never forgotten the mythological figures from ancient Greece, which had been revived in a symbolic if depressing way by Böcklin. But, if there were heads in his work before and during most of the war, he abolished features or at least eyes. There is still a plaster head in the portrait of Apollinaire, but the poet's profile appears only as a silhouette, while two other paintings of 1914 include a faintly female figure draped in a tunic but showing a head with no features and only an indication for the eyes – the head of a tailor's dummy, a mannequin. The idea for these half-human figures is thought to have come from a curious piece that Savinio published in *Les Soirées de Paris* just before the outbreak of war: 'Les Chants de la mi-mort' – 'The Songs of Half-Death' – in which there appeared a figure 'without voice, without eyes or face'. This link was first suggested by the critic Raffaello Carrieri in a 1942 essay about the painter and was described by James Thrall Soby in his 1955 book about de Chirico after Savinio himself had confirmed that it was accurate.

If de Chirico eliminated living humanity from most of his painting, as he was to do now in so much of his output during the Ferrara years, it was not through lack of people in his life. Although his correspondence shows that he missed his few Paris friends and wanted to receive any periodicals with news of painters and writers, he now found new friends in Italy. Among them, he later remembered the young Filippo de Pisis, who wrote, studied and sketched before becoming a painter. De Chirico was fascinated by the way de Pisis lived, surrounded by 'heteroclite' objects which formed a kind of surrealist background, a 'magician's laboratory'. No doubt such conditions would never have been tolerated by de Chirico's mother, but they may have influenced him in some way, for his paintings began to fill with motifs that had never appeared in the paintings of the Paris years. Long after meeting this young man he could still refer to him as a 'genius' and describe how he wore a smock 'like Maxim Gorky' – although not in the photograph taken of the two men together, showing de Chirico in his drab corporal's uniform. Apparently they discussed the German philosophers they had both studied, de Chirico wrote poetry and de Pisis wrote the first article about his friend's work to appear in Italy. It was all a long way from the Western Front and the 'war' on conventional art and writing that was being prepared by Tristan Tzara and his friends in Switzerland, the explosive movement of Dada.

No one could have been further from Dada than the poet and painter Corrado Govoni, whom de Chirico also met. He was a recluse who did not often receive visitors, especially if they called on him when he was asleep, as de Chirico described in a short poem published later in his brother's book *Hermaphrodito*. It is as prosaic as the poem he wrote about the death of his eccentric uncle, but it evokes the kind of atmosphere he liked:

> He is acclaimed in the city by three thousand statues on pedestals
>   so low they seem to walk along with the shivering citizens.
> On the stage all is mystery . . .
> The looking-glass on the easel. The painting is not yet complete.
> The philosopher is sleeping. A knock at the door.

Apparently the two men enjoyed each other's company so much that de Chirico stayed in Govoni's house for a time, although he does not mention this in his *Memoirs*.

He continued to paint. Ferrara seemed to stimulate him, just as the outbreak of war had enlivened Cocteau in 1914. The beauty of the old city had impressed him, he wrote, but he seems to have been less interested now in arcades and squares (although he did not forget them entirely) and he began to move inside: 'what struck me most of all and inspired me on the metaphysical side, the manner in which I was working then, were certain aspects of Ferrara interiors'. Writing in 1945, he insisted, as he always did after 1925 or so, that he had continued to paint such 'so-called metaphysical interiors' – 'with some variations' – and still painted them.

Walking about the streets, he also noticed 'certain windows, shops, houses, districts, such as the ancient ghetto, where you could find certain sweets and biscuits with remarkably metaphysical and strange shapes'. 'How can biscuits have "metaphysical" shapes?' newcomers to de Chirico's work will ask. In one way they were merely shapes, but perhaps in another way the painter used them to introduce a sign of humanity into his work, for sweets and biscuits are for eating – he was still creating links between the real and the unreal. The surrealists later were particularly impressed by these images, to which Breton refers in his *Surrealism and Painting*. At the end of the 1960s the artist was asked why he had chosen to paint them; he replied in an offhand way that he had liked the shapes and they contrasted well with the dark-blue background he had used for some of them at the time.

During the war Ferrara supplied him with the atmosphere he needed: it was 'the city of surprises'; it possessed, he wrote in 1920, a spectral and subtle beauty; there were memories of Ariosto, there was a theatrical atmosphere, a lingering sense of the Middle Ages, an alchemist's laboratory . . . What more could he have wanted? He never forgot Turin, but Ferrara was even more important to him.

Although he complained about his military duties, he found time and energy now to paint some of his most impressive works. These included a wide range of motifs. Many use a picture within a picture to display maps or factories in miniature, while even more include drawing instruments such as T-squares – perhaps a distant memory of those owned by his father. For the biographer the most intriguing paintings are those that seem to indicate a changed way of looking at people – presentations of a half-human element; heads that are either made of solid wood or appear hollow with elongated arcade shapes for eyes. *The Soothsayer* of 1915 gazes unseeingly at a blackboard behind which is a mysterious shadow while on the board is a sketch with converging lines, possibly a room in perspective. Sometimes two different heads appear, one solid, one not, as in *The Two Sisters* (1915) or *The Two Masks* (possibly 1916). But the most arresting paintings are those that show some sexual differentiation, such as *The Duo* (1915) or the impressive *Hector and Andromache* of 1917, although the figures are still dummies, as though constructed of pieces of wood suitably carved and then nailed together. In *The Duo* the two half-human or mythological figures stand close together like a danseur and a ballerina about to take up a position from classical ballet, but they have no arms: as dancers or would-be humans they are more than limited. If the smaller figure on the left is meant to be female, she looks uncertain and dejected. Two similar figures in the *Hector and Andromache* paintings – one of 1917, another probably of the same year – are almost human and seem almost ready to embrace: their heads touch. Maybe de Chirico found it easier to present figures from mythology: perhaps he regarded them as having lived a kind of metaphysical life.

Some thirty years later it may have been the paintings of this period that made a deep impression on the English writer Geoffrey Grigson and led him to compose a poem of seven stanzas in honour of de Chirico. The title, 'The New Dummy', may not be very flattering, but the poet seems to have understood the essence of the painter's message:

> A sad painter of the green midnight,
>   Perspectives past the dark arcade,
> Set in an immense twilight
>   His moleskin squares of shade;

And then a man without a face,
Mechanically self-made.

This dummy man, this blade of brilliant tacks,
Stands there with parabolic thighs,
And bends a head which lacks,
But seems to recollect, its eyes;
And in this lyrical parade seems sad
Because he cannot summon up surprise.

Two mysterious paintings, *The Jewish Angel* and *Greetings from a Distant Friend*, both of 1916, include a motif said to be part of an eye. But in an impressive painting of 1917, *The Disquieting Muses*, the barely feminine forms have no eyes – in fact no faces: they are half-mannequins, half-statues, and one, who is seated, appears to have removed her 'head' and placed it on the ground beside her. This work mystified and attracted so many people that the painter made several later versions of it, the last dating possibly from 1947.

In addition to painting, de Chirico was writing both poetry and prose; he also corresponded with Giovanni Papini and with Tristan Tzara in Zurich. News from Paris during the war years was mixed. Paul Guillaume reopened his gallery in 1915 and showed some of the paintings de Chirico had left either with the dealer or in his old studio. In early February 1916 Apollinaire visited Paris during a forty-eight-hour leave and is said to have been shocked at the uncaring atmosphere of the capital, where most people still regarded the war as something unpleasant happening a long way away. A month or so later, on 17 March, when the poet was on active service in the Aisne region in north-east France, he was wounded in the head when a shell exploded near by. Shrapnel was removed during surgery, but early in May paralysis set in and, in order to prevent it spreading, trepanation was carried out. De Chirico's 1914 portrait of the poet had included a silhouette-profile with a mysterious white circle round the left eye and temple; this was close to the site of the wound, and the painting now seemed prophetic.

Apollinaire was not discharged from the army and was soon well enough to visit Paris again, where he was posted to censorship work and then to the Ministry for the Colonies. On 13 November he gave a lecture at Paul Guillaume's gallery, and a photograph taken of him there shows de Chirico's painting *The Prince's Toys* (thought to date from 1915) standing on the floor against the wall behind him. In the meantime, according to Maurizio Fagiolo dell'Arco, three paintings by de Chirico were shown at an exhibition arranged by Guillaume and the writer André Salmon. They were hung in prestigious company – that of Derain, Léger, Matisse and the Italian Severini, while Picasso's *Demoiselles d'Avignon*, which apparently had previously been seen only by a few friends in the artist's studio, was the most famous, or infamous, painting to be shown.

De Chirico was still fascinated by Ferrara, and since he was there for nearly three years, from 1915 to 1918, he had time to look round and think in more detail about the city and its inhabitants. In addition to de Pisis and Govoni, he either knew or knew of several other eccentrics, and some of them appeared in his later writing. He regarded the Ferrarese as suffering from 'latent madness' and thought them 'terribly lecherous; there are days, especially at the height of spring, in which the libidinous atmosphere that hangs over Ferrara becomes so strong that it can almost be heard'. The atmosphere was thought to be due to the fumes from the hemp harvest and the humidity rising from the surrounding marshes, and de Chirico even quoted Baudelaire on the 'vertiginous spirit' rising out of this crop.

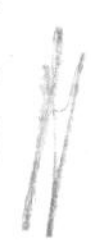

Savinio was fascinated too and saw Ferrara as 'the city of a thousand natural mysteries'. His descriptions of the famous sweets and biscuits in the little shops are as amusingly colourful as his remarks about the women of the city: they were 'frightening. They wear their animal-like beauty imprinted on their faces, like a disease.' He became surrealist: 'They have eyes like those of a crayfish: small lucid globes, like those of laxative pills, sprouting from the tip of a corneal antenna.' He believed that these eyes enabled the women to see sideways and even to see what was happening behind them.

There was a biographical rumour, as I call such unsubstantiated statements, that de Chirico himself found a woman friend in Ferrara and even became half-engaged. It is not known if she was Ferrarese or not, but she was said to be '*très bien*'. However, she did not please the Baronessa, who no doubt still saw herself as the only woman in the life of her sons, and the relationship ended. One Ferrarese woman was mentioned by the painter in his recollections: Corrado Govoni's beautiful wife, who possessed 'that "nocturnal gaze" and those special eyes which are characteristic of some women of Ferrara'. She earned this tribute because she gave the thirsty soldier a drink made from real tamarind syrup.

In Ferrara madness was in the air – or it might be fairer to say that in the Italian army there were now many cases of mental disturbance, occurring in two ways: as a result of shell-shock through being in action and as a result of either fear of action or simply depression or anxiety due to frustration and lack of action. It so happened that cases of both types were treated at the Villa del Seminario, a former convent, then a hospital and convalescent home, just outside the city. During the early months of 1917 the medical staff there received three new cases: the two de Chirico brothers and the futurist painter Carlo Carrà.

Why were they there? There seems no obvious reason for Savinio's presence: he did not stay long and was soon sent to Macedonia for a year as an interpreter, although he complained that his knowledge of languages was never needed. De Chirico himself was probably depressed by war conditions, which, although they had not prevented him from painting, limited the possibility of selling his work; his partly psychosomatic intestinal troubles also seem to have recurred, and he was not physically fit for service at the front. His first wife later said that he feigned mental illness in order to escape active service, but that was easily said, especially since she did not know him at the time.

Carlo Carrà was seven years older than de Chirico and had had a very different life. Born in Piedmont, he had left home when he was only twelve and had worked for several years as a mural painter. Later he studied in Milan, and in 1909 he became one of the original signatories to Marinetti's futurist manifesto. Many of his futurist paintings were impressive – *The Funeral of the Anarchist Galli* (1911), for instance, or *The Red Horseman* (1913) – but after a time he distanced himself from the movement and began to produce collages. Like de Chirico, he also enjoyed writing: he produced articles, including discussions of Giotto and Uccello, and also wrote poems and semi-philosophical works about art. He would have been a hypocrite if he had remained a futurist, for he no longer shared their creed or their vision, and by 1916, the year of his *Drunken Gentleman*, he had already moved into a different world – closer, in fact, to the world of metaphysical painting.

There were several legends which may explain why Carlo Carrà arrived at Il Seminario. Soon after joining the army he is said to have made a serious mistake: he gave his captain a copy of his book of aggressive sketches, *Guerrapittura*, signed 'Carrààà' for emphasis. The captain was shocked, and it is said that as a punishment he caused Carrà to be committed to the mental hospital. Another legend is more colourful and probably also untrue. When asked to paint a portrait of his commanding officer on horseback he did so – it should be remembered that the image of a horseman had occurred in many of Carrà's paintings. The officer had presumably hoped for a portrait that was lifelike or perhaps even idealized; but what he received was neither, and his reaction was predictable in the terms of this surely apocryphal story: the artist was certainly insane, he decided, and must therefore be committed to the Villa del Seminario.

Carrà and de Chirico were not 'mad'; they were depressed and confused, worrying about their future – if there was to be any. Within a decade or so the surrealists, who were now forming, so to speak, would be seriously discussing the relationship between madness and creativity, studying work by the clinically insane. André Breton had not yet given up medical studies, but after working at the front as a nurse and paramedic he had been disturbed by soldier-patients suffering from some forms of shell-shock, like the 'mental cases' that the English poet Wilfred Owen wrote about. He had become closely interested in psychology and psychiatry, although he had failed to persuade Apollinaire to take them equally seriously.

No one was to condemn such 'sciences' more angrily than de

Chirico when in later life he constantly attacked all forms of 'modernism', but for the time being he could not complain about his stay in the hospital, which was said to be the most modern of its kind in Europe. The director was a Dr Gaetano Boschi, who had the rank of major, and he made use of all the latest methods of treatment: special 'therapeutic' baths, walks in the countryside, sailing expeditions and work of a suitable kind. The patients were never locked in their rooms at night, and the charitable ladies of Ferrara had donated such useful items as a piano, games, magazines, comfortable sofas and decorative plants. Carrà and de Chirico were allowed to 'work', that is, to paint, using former convent cells on the top floor as studios. There were no easels: they stood their canvases on chairs.

They probably did not meet for the first time in the Villa del Seminario. The futurist writer and painter Ardengo Soffici had put them in touch earlier, and de Chirico had written to Carrà, addressing him as *tu* in what appears to have been his first letter and describing how he and his brother had tried to locate him in the barracks. The two men worked close to each other in Il Seminario from late April to August in 1917, and their very different paintings included the same images – mannequin figures, architectural motifs, blackboards, maps, pictures within a picture. Although Carrà was an experienced painter, he could not have invented by accident all the same themes used by his temporary colleague, but he was to claim that he had already produced 'metaphysical' work earlier, and he was soon to write about it. Nobody could possibly be mistaken about the paintings on similar themes the two men produced: the technique and the atmosphere are totally different. Dr Boschi remembered the two men as different – Carrà was the brilliant and talkative extrovert; de Chirico was *chiuso*, withdrawn, and said very little.

The two men seemed close; they planned a joint exhibition of metaphysical work at the Chini Gallery in Milan; they wrote passages of poetic prose dedicated to each other. Then the unexpected happened. De Chirico asserted in his *Memoirs* that his fellow patient, 'with something of a struggle', began to paint 'the same subjects that I was doing, and all this with an effrontery and a *sans gêne* that were truly astonishing'. De Chirico went on to describe how Carrà 'then procured a longer period of convalescence' and went to Milan, 'taking with him the metaphysical paintings he had done at the Ferrara convalescent home'. Carrà's show was held at the Chini Gallery in December 1917. De Chirico was left out, and later, in his 1943 autobiography, the older man mentioned him only casually in a list of names. If the word 'enigma' had disappeared now from de Chirico's work, a different kind of enigma had taken its place, and there seems no way of proving what happened in the Villa del Seminario, although it does look as though his description of the incident was largely correct. Compared to the general tone of his remarks about other painters he seems uncharacteristically restrained here, but I suspect that the change in his relationship with Carrà was the beginning of de Chirico's resentful, distrustful attitude that was to deepen as time went on – so much so that he became virtually paranoid.

De Chirico left Il Seminario the following year, but he was not in good shape: he was examined at another hospital, declared unfit for active service and told to take life quietly, which he did for a time, before he then returned to painting. He had to move into lodgings, for his mother appears to have gone to Rome, probably after Savinio had been sent to Macedonia. In the meantime his work was becoming more widely known, and in Zurich some of it was shown at the 1917 Dada exhibition, accompanied by praise from Tristan Tzara, who spoke of de Chirico's imagination covering us 'with green ice; he takes abstraction towards poisonous and mystical irony'.

The painter began to write more, publishing texts of various kinds, including surrealist prose, and even drew caricatures, some of which were published in the army magazine *La Ghirba*, edited by Ardengo Soffici. He met Mario Broglio, a journalist and keen collector of paintings (also a fat man who loved eating), and his impressive prose piece 'Zeuxis the Explorer' appeared in the first issue of Broglio's review *Valori Plastici*, published from 1918 to 1922. He also wrote a piece expressing the hope that in future Italian art would be fully recognized, that France would not dominate the art world and that a new European attitude would develop.

The war ended with an outbreak of Spanish flu which killed no fewer than 25 million people. It killed Apollinaire, and it might have killed de Chirico, who was sent back to Il Seminario at the worst of the epidemic in the autumn of 1918, but he claimed that his use of old proven remedies and a little bribery of the staff cured him. During his convalescence he was once more nurtured by the single person on whom he could rely – his mother. He summoned her back from Rome, and when he was fit, in the winter of 1918, they returned there together.

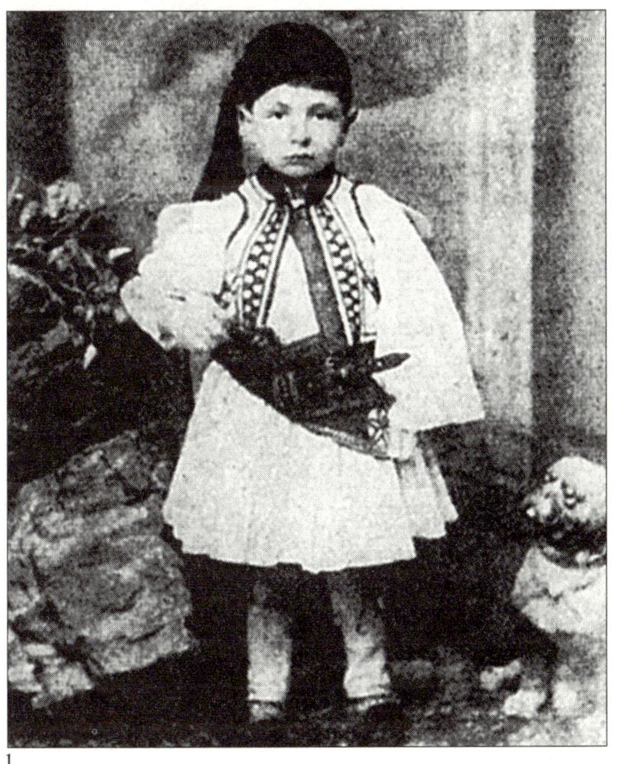

1

Giorgio de Chirico at four years of age in Greek evzone costume

2 Evaristo and Gemma de Chirico outside their villa in Greece, 1897, with Giorgio on the left and Andrea in the middle

3 Giorgio with his mother, Gemma de Chirico, and his sister Adèle, Athens, 1890

4 Evaristo de Chirico, Giorgio's father

5 Giorgio de Chirico while at the Munich Academy, 1908

6 A meeting of surrealists at the home of Simone Breton in 1925. From left to right: Max Morise, Pierre Naville, Jacques Baron, André Breton, Paul Eluard, Giorgio de Chirico, Francis Gérard, Louis Aragon, Charles Baron and Robert Desnos. The photograph was probably taken by Man Ray.

Reproduced from the exhibition catalogue *Le Surréalisme 1922–1942*, Musée des Arts Décoratifs, Paris, 9 June–24 September 1972

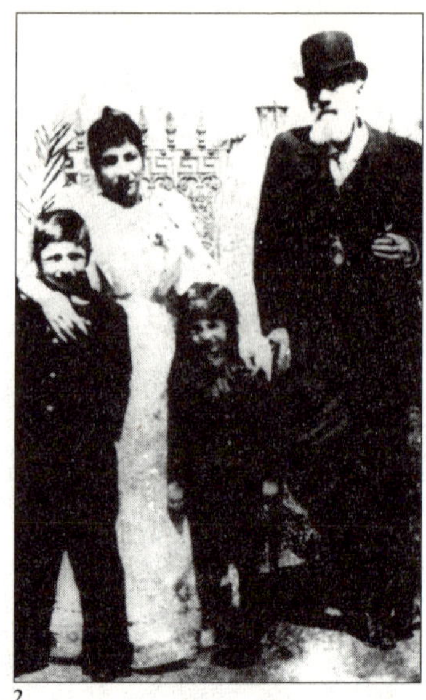

2

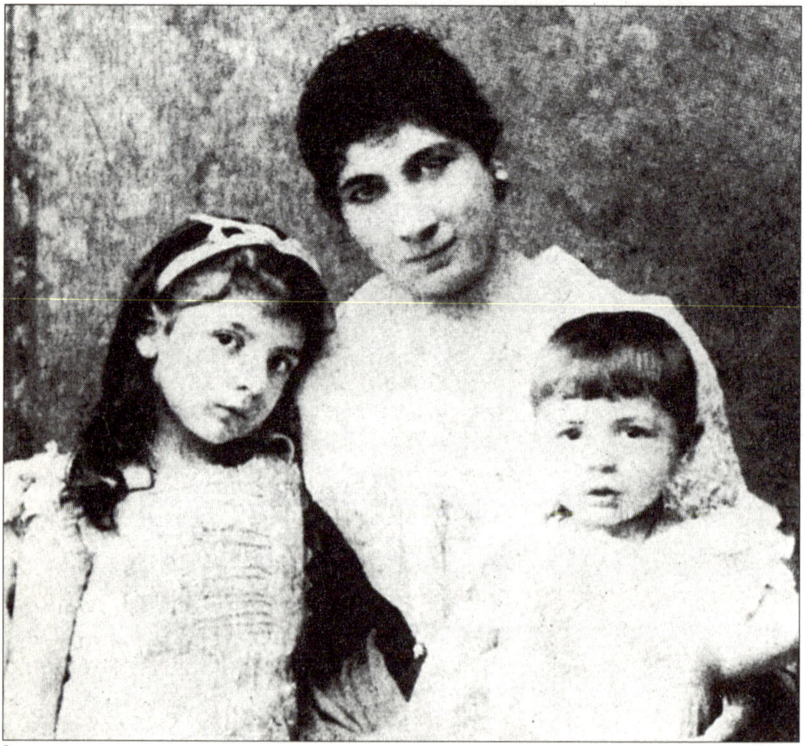

3

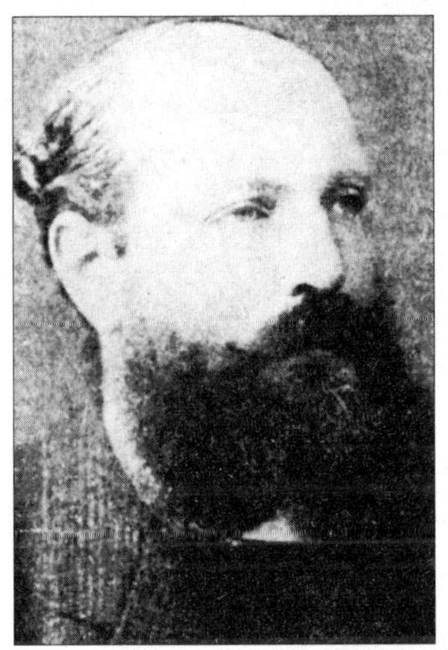
4

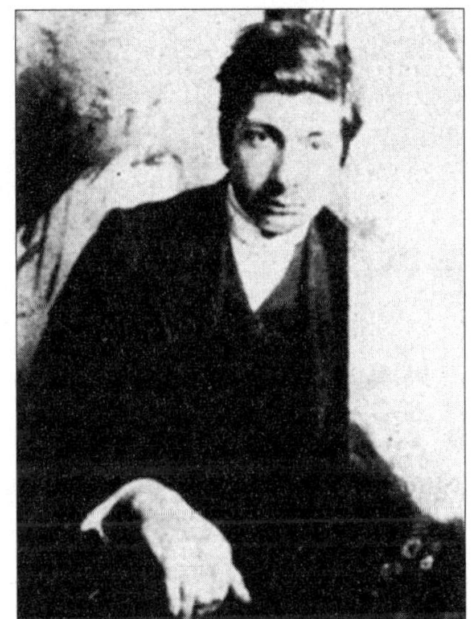
5

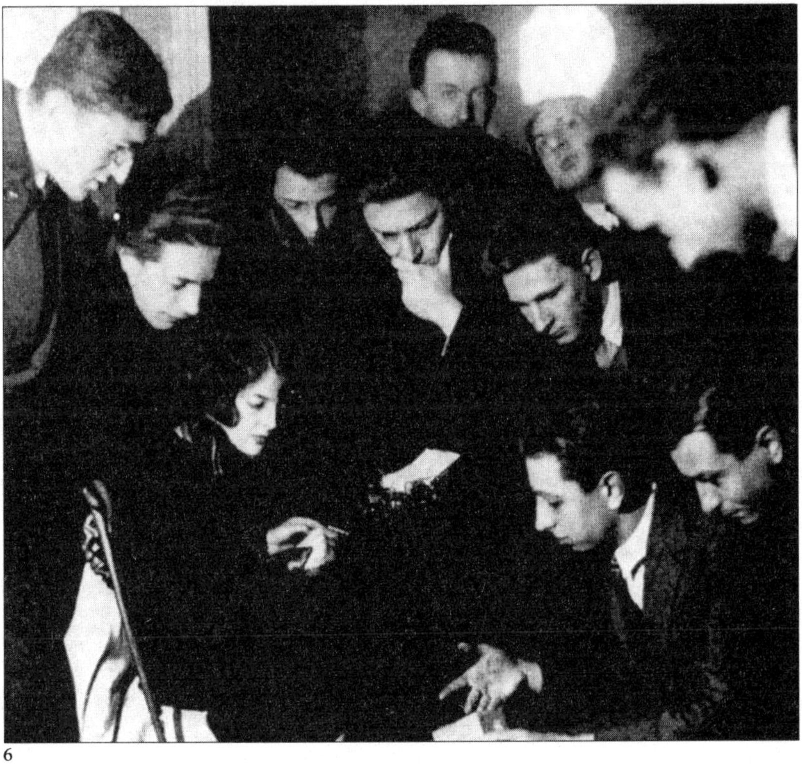

6

7 De Chirico and his first wife Raissa, *c.* 1926

8 De Chirico in Paris, 1930

9, 10 Two views of de Chirico working on a large mural, Milan, 1933

11 De Chirico in a street in Rome immediately after the Second World War

7

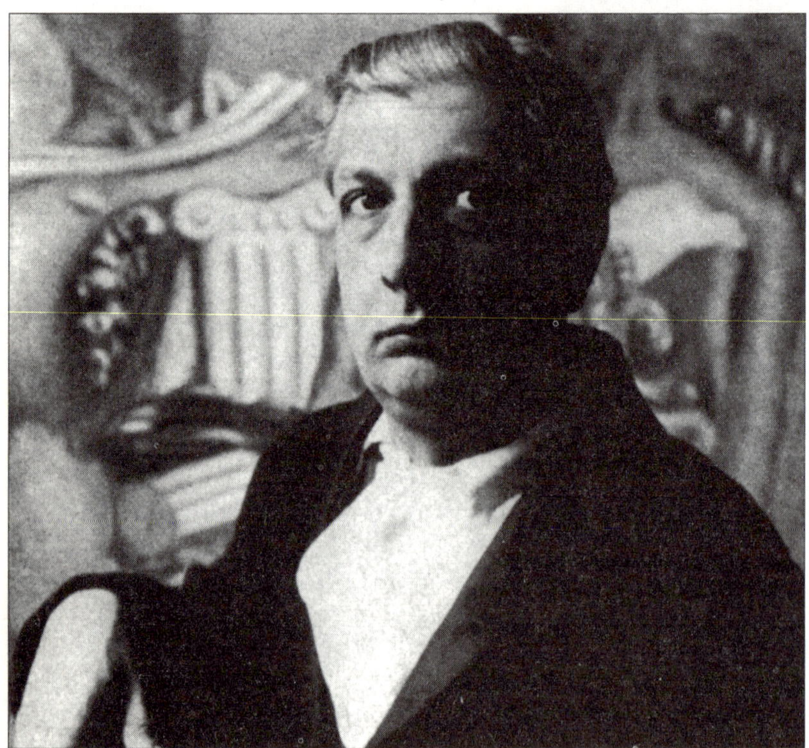

8

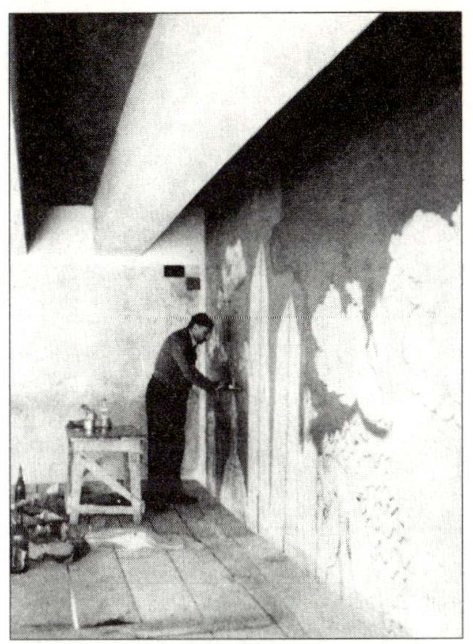
9

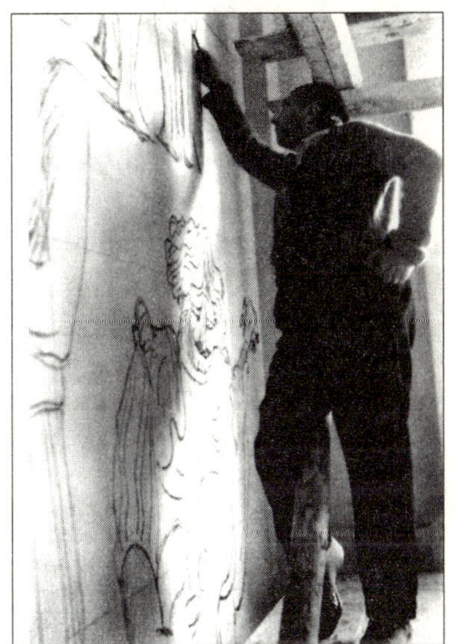
10

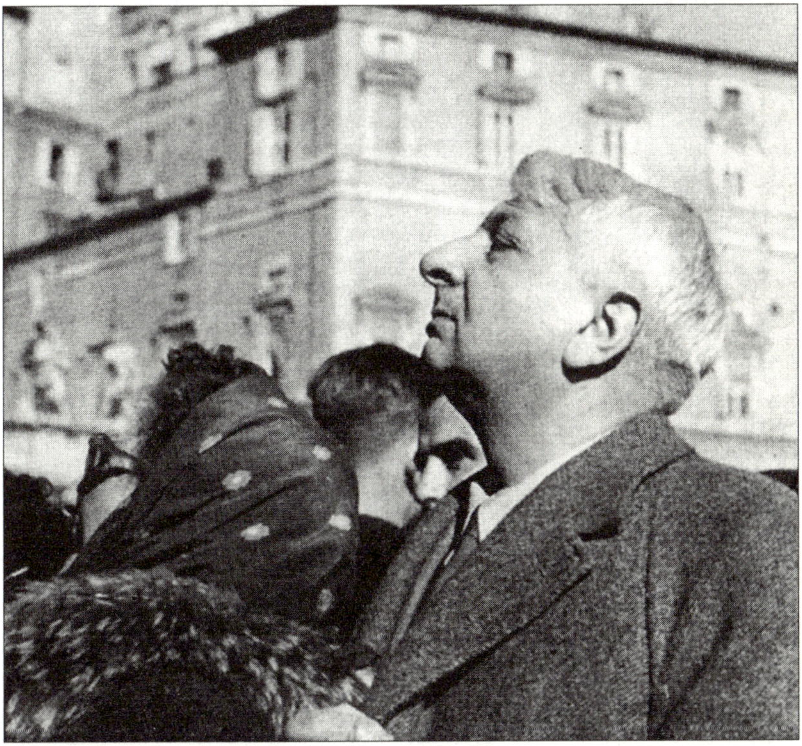

11

12 De Chirico in front of *Nude Self-Portrait*, 1945 to which a loincloth was added on the occasion of the Royal Academy exhibition, London, 1949

Reproduced from *Catalogo Generale*, 1981

13 De Chirico and his second wife Isabella Far at home, 1961

Reproduced from *Stylbert Moda*, November 1961

14 De Chirico and Isabella in the dining-room of their apartment in Rome, 1968

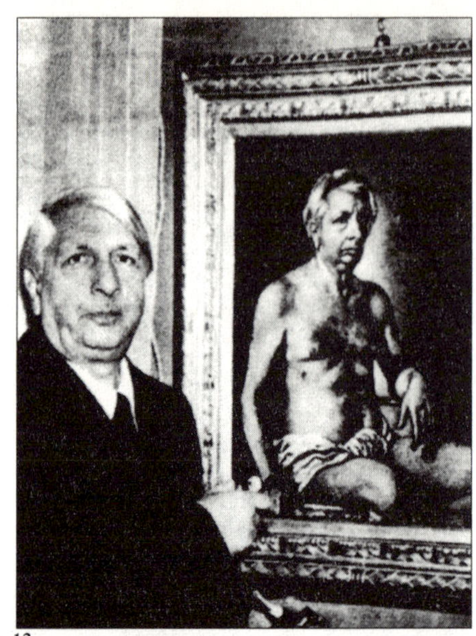

12

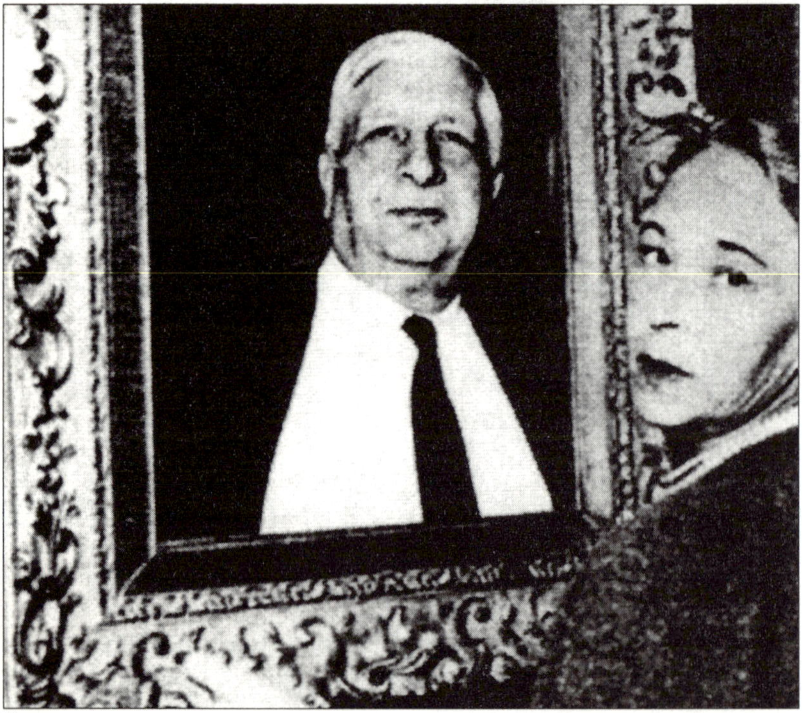

13

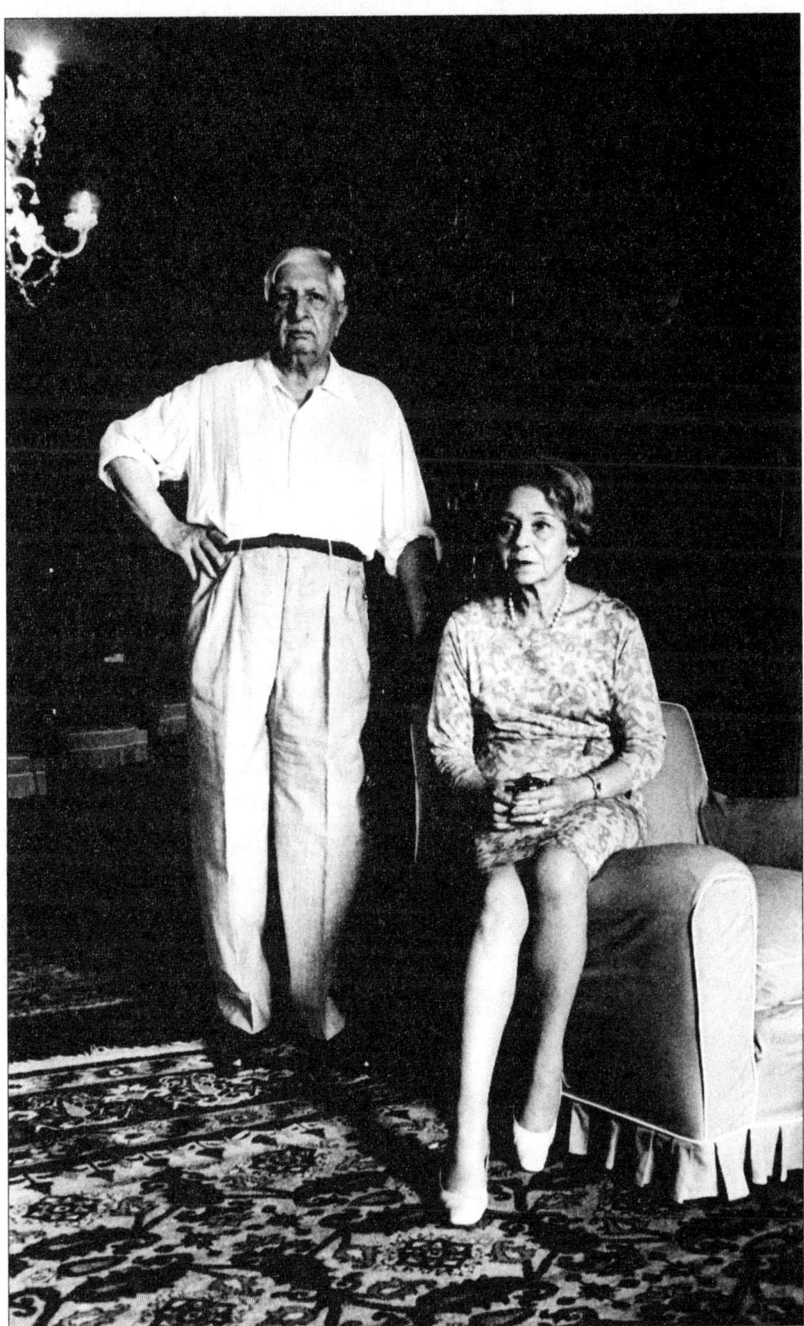

14

15 In his house in Rome

16 De Chirico and Isabella outside their villa near Rome

17 De Chirico in his apartment, Rome, 1968

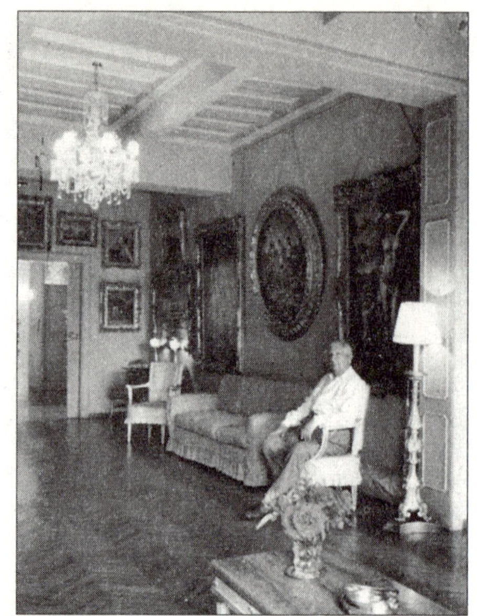

15

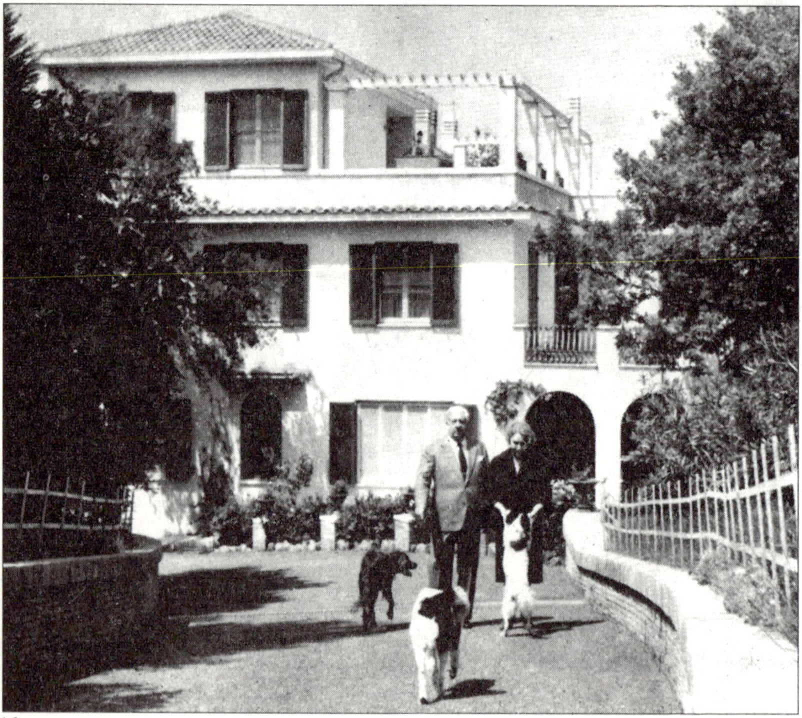

16

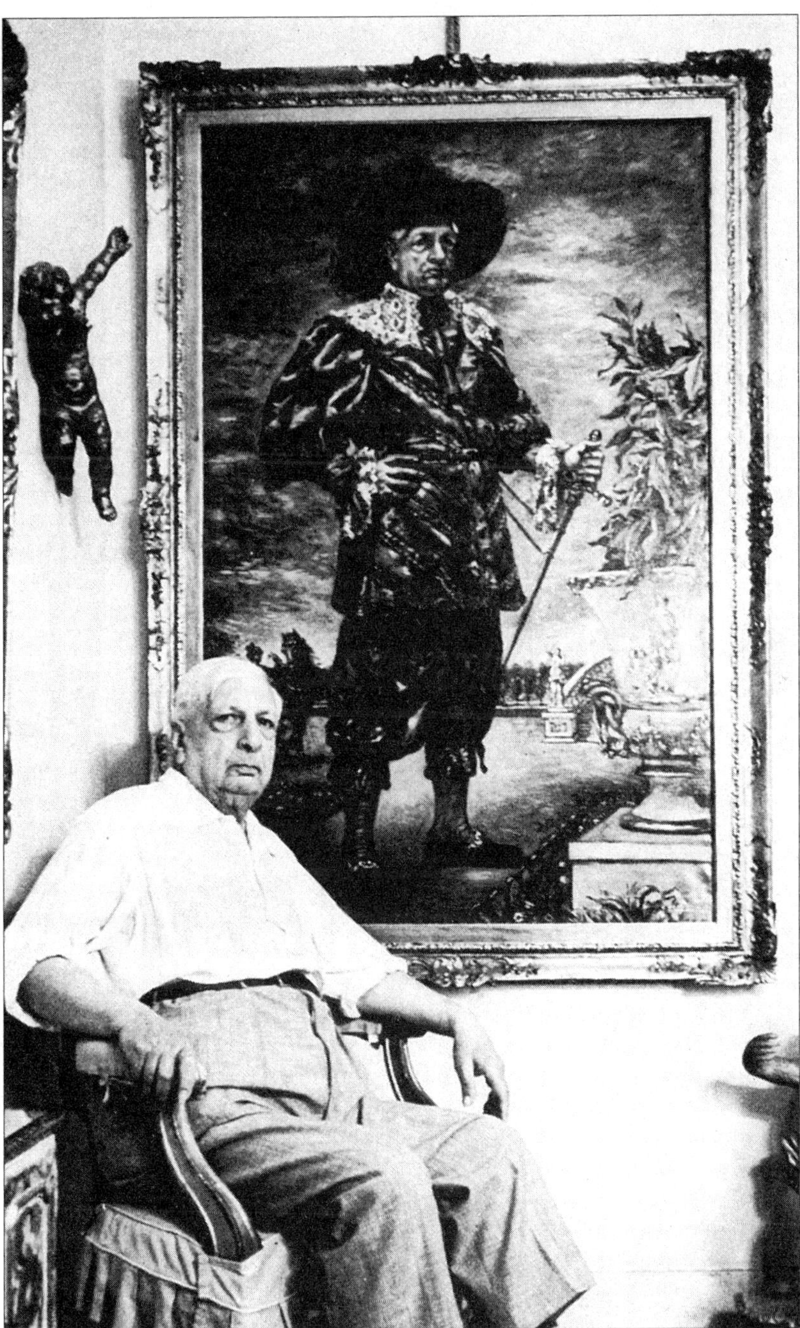

17

18 De Chirico on the occasion of his reception into the Académie des Beaux-Arts, Paris, 11 June 1975

19 The artist in his studio

20 Painting at his studio in the Piazza di Spagna, Rome

Reproduced from *L'Epoca*, May 1970

21 Working in his Rome studio modelling horses in clay

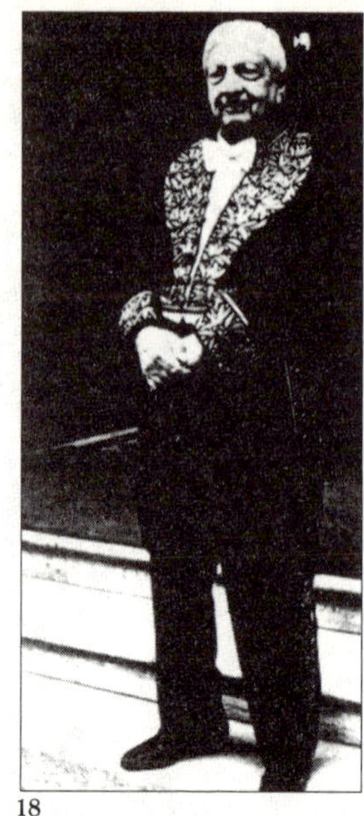

18

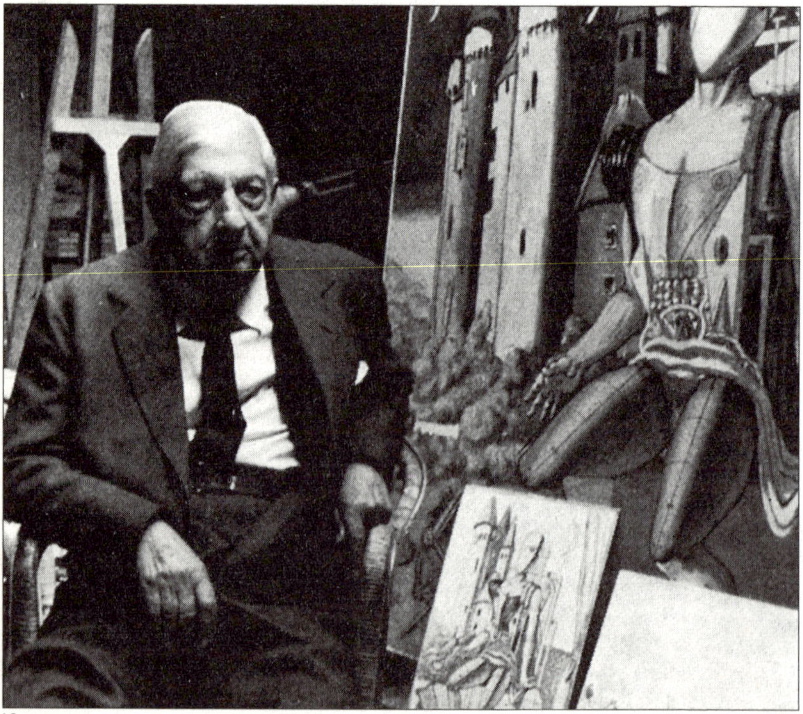

19

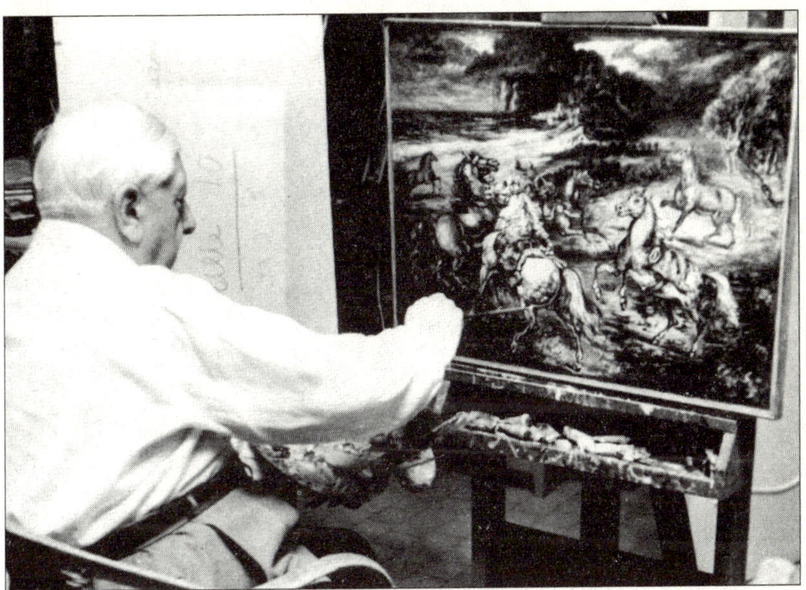

20

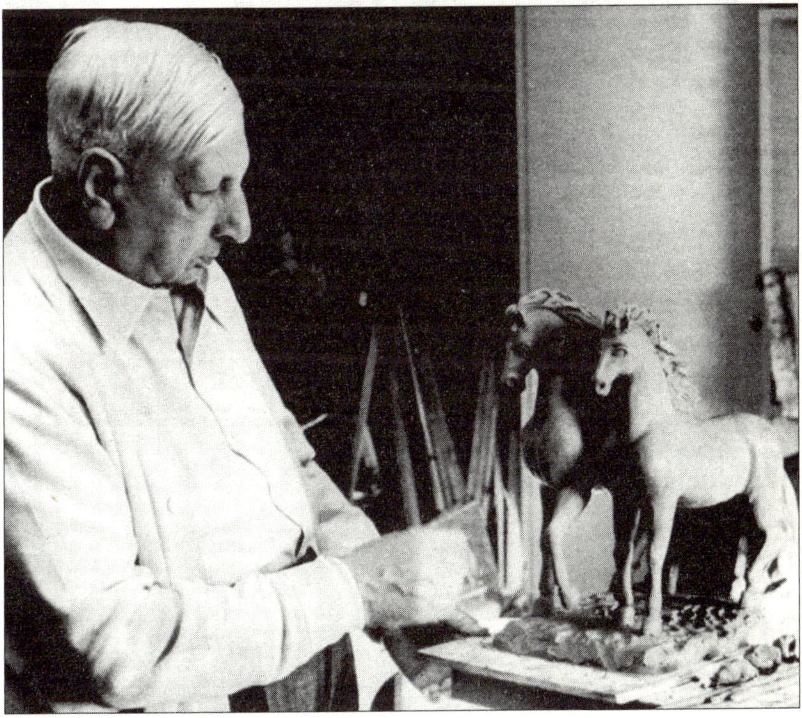

21

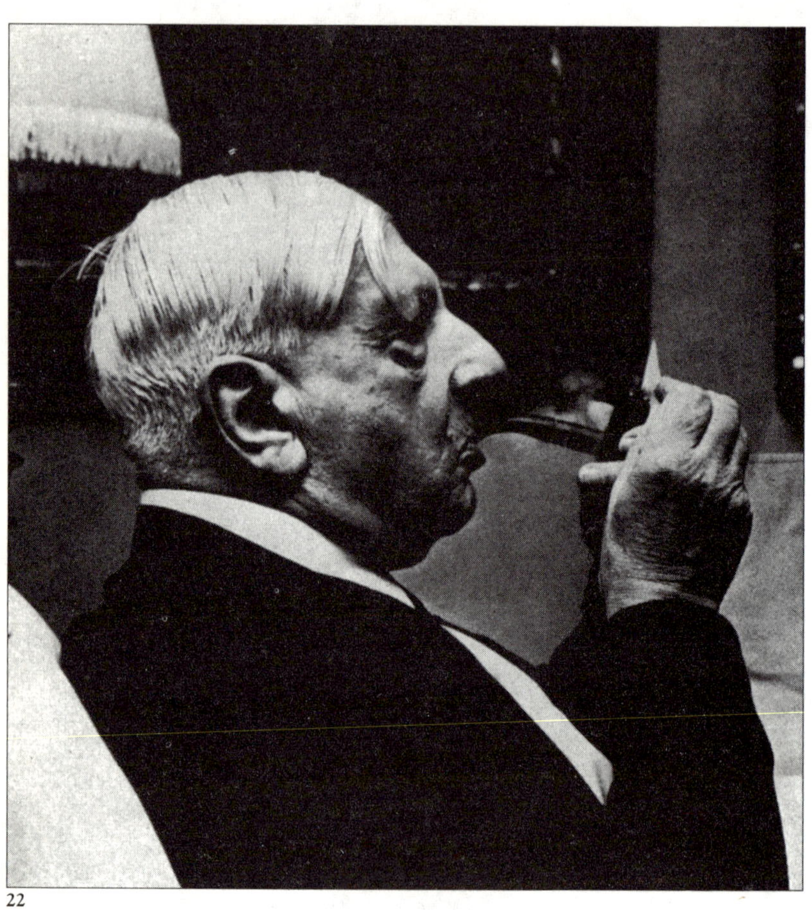

22

De Chirico in later life

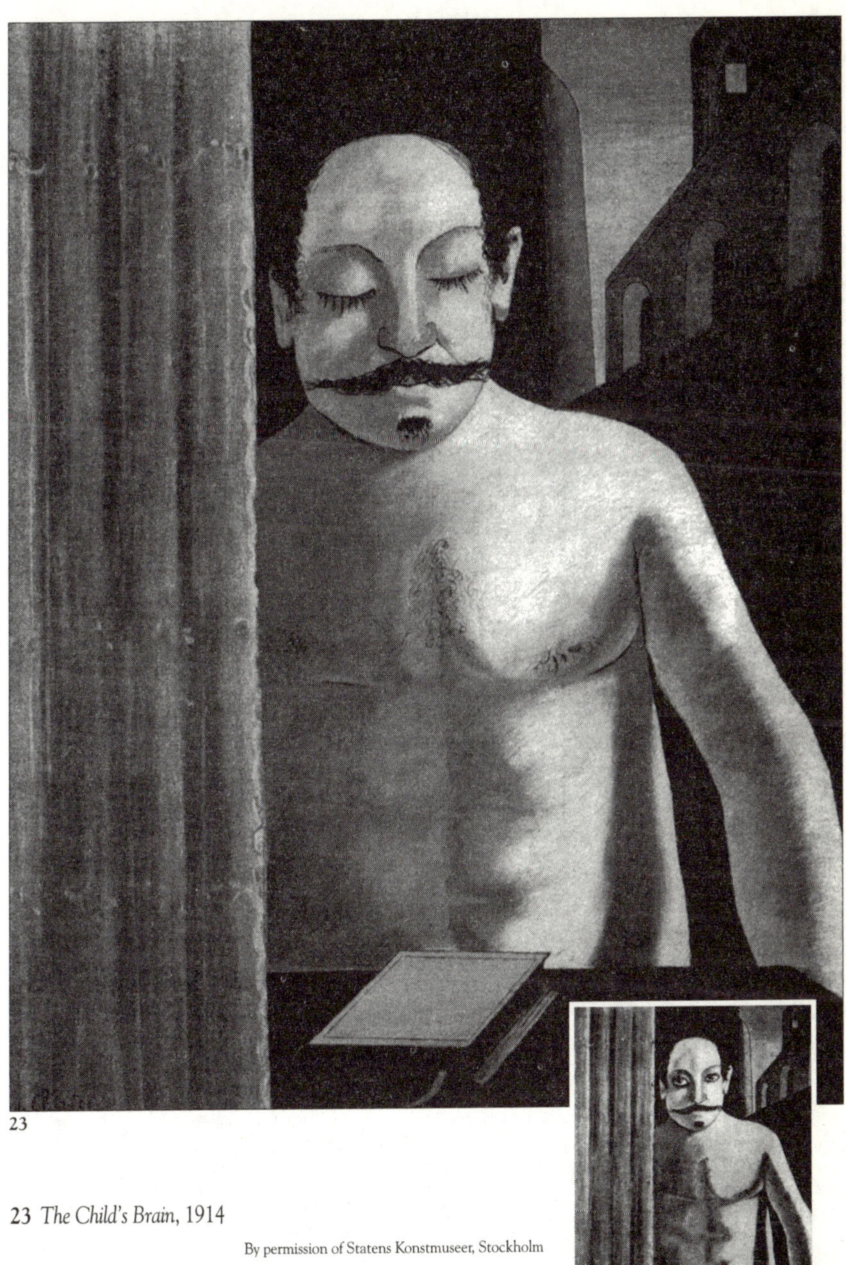

23

24

23 *The Child's Brain*, 1914

By permission of Statens Konstmuseer, Stockholm

24 *The Reawakening of the Child's Brain*, André Breton, 1950

Almanach Surréaliste du Demi Siècle

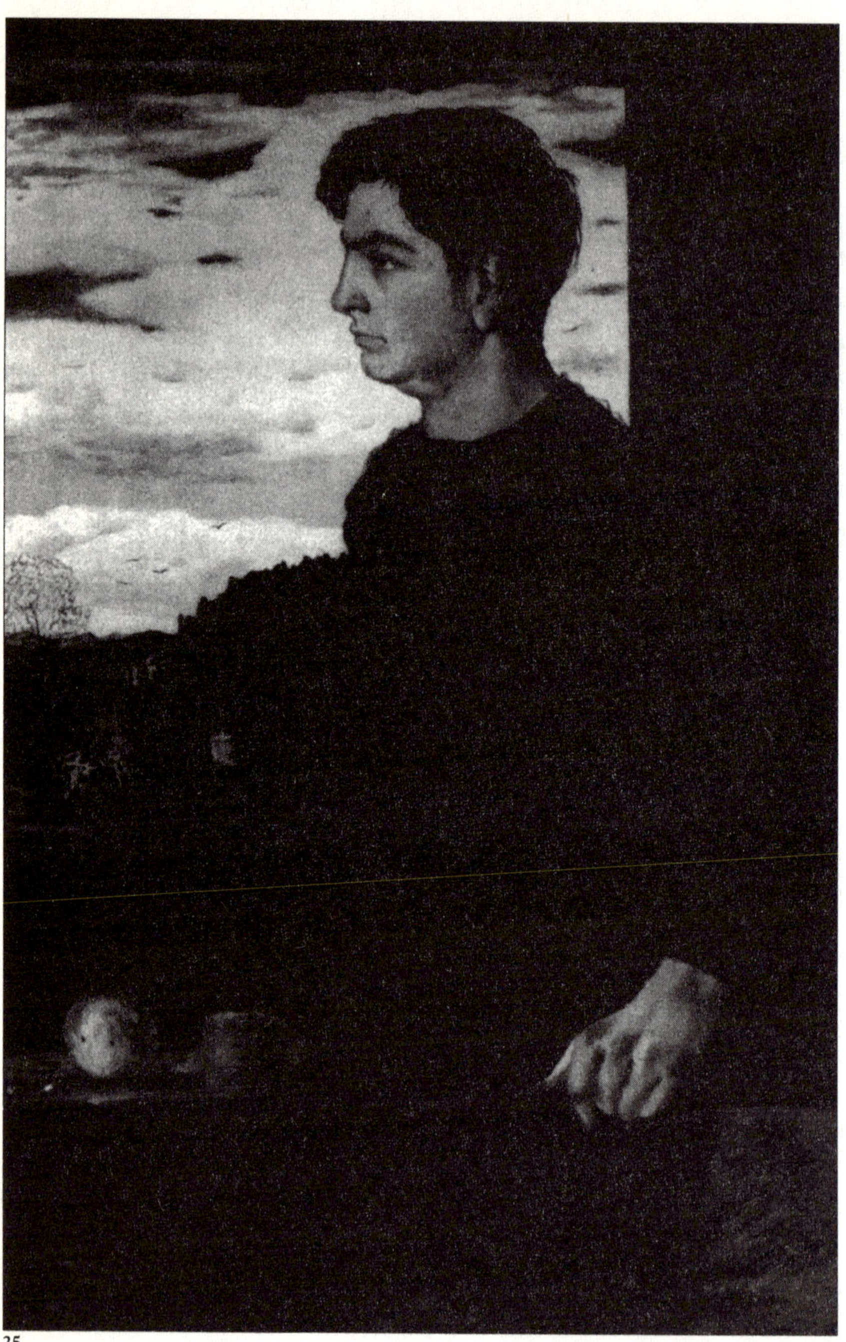

25

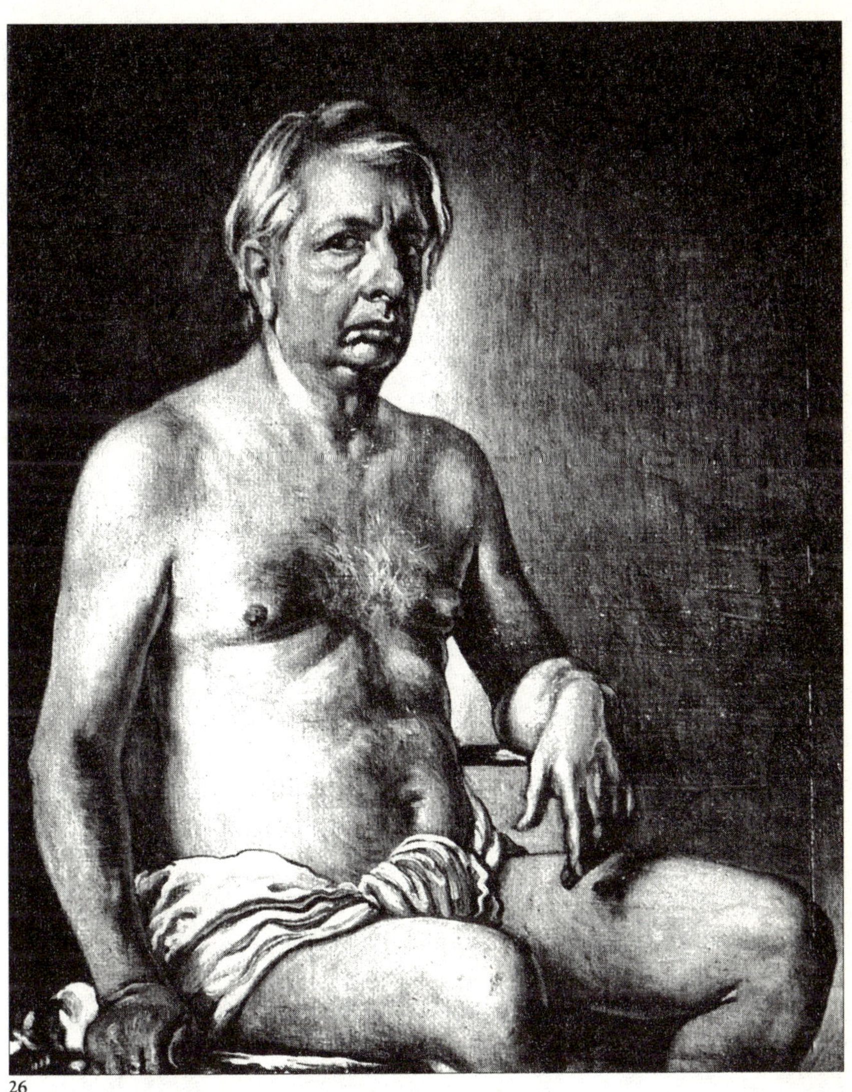

26

25 *Portrait of Andrea de Chirico*, 1910, Giorgio's younger brother also known as Alberto Savinio

By permission of Staatliche Museen, Berlin

26 *Nude Self-Portrait*, 1945

Formerly in the private collection of G. and I. de Chirico

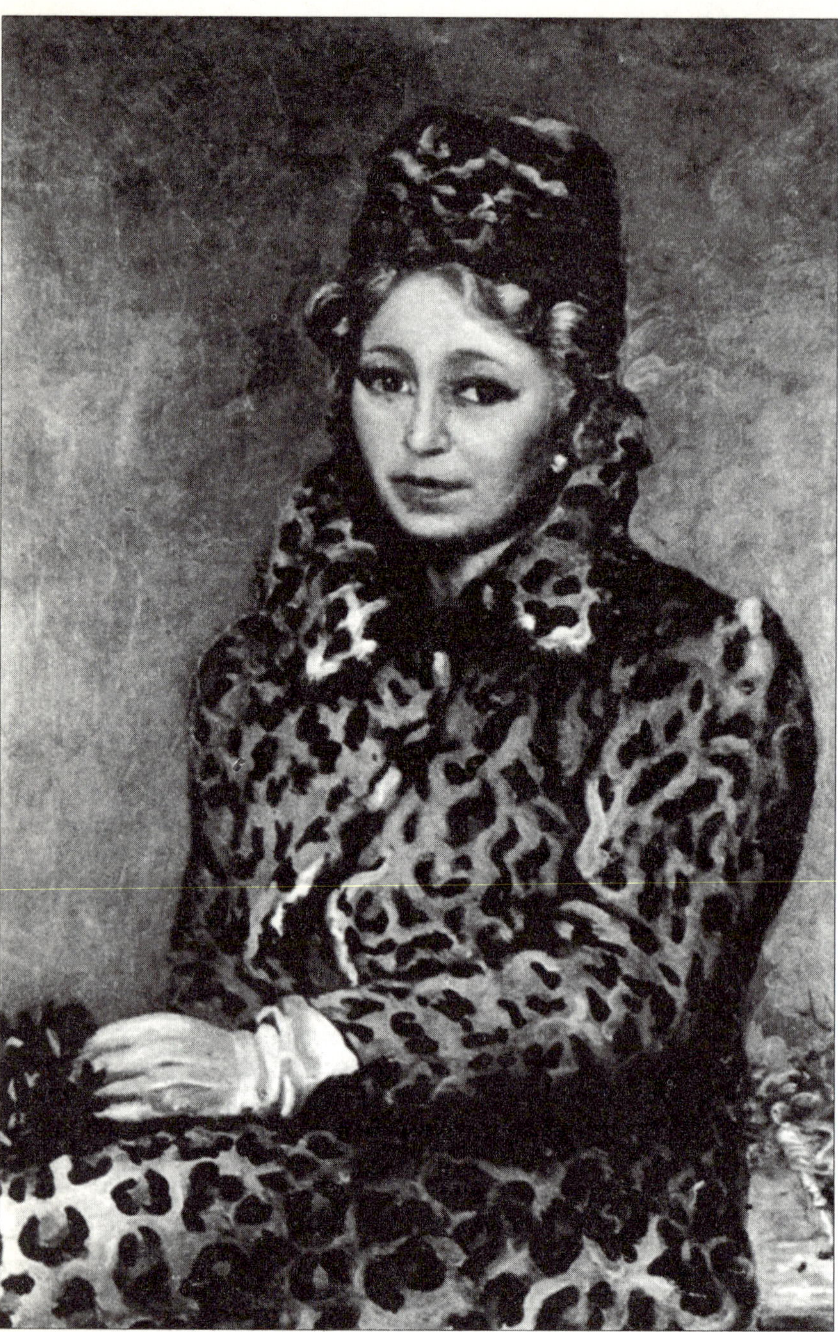

27

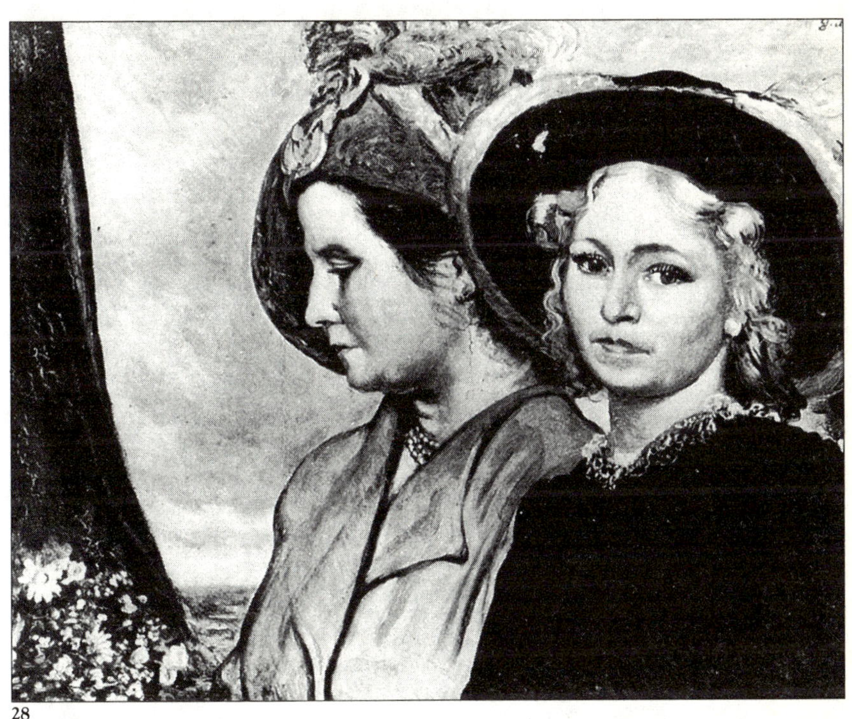

28

27 Portrait of Isabella. Painting known as *The Skater*, 1941

Formerly in the private collection of G. and I. de Chirico

28 Isabella on the right and her sister-in-law Maria Savinio. Painting known as *The Sisters-in-Law*, c. 1941

Formerly in the private collection of G. and I. de Chirico

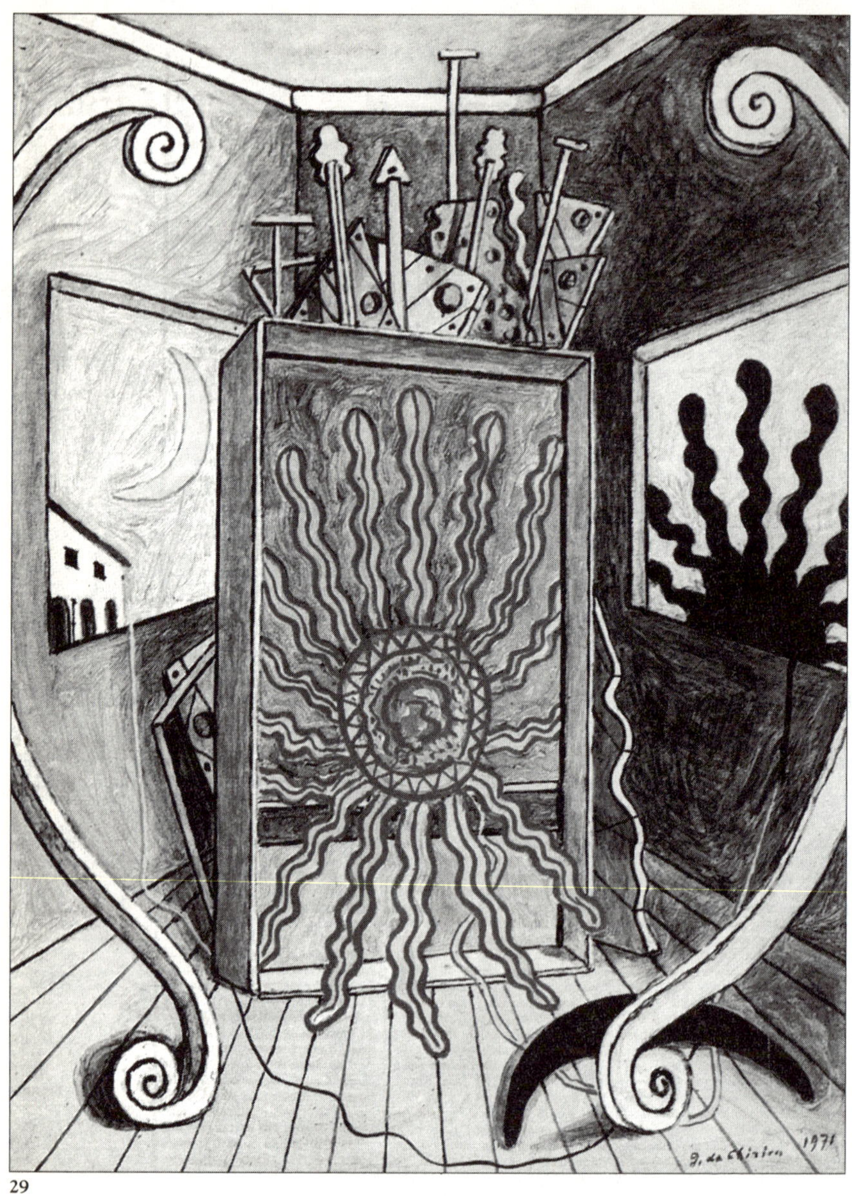

29

The Sun Entering a Metaphysical Interior, 1971, inspired by de Chirico's earlier illustrations of poems by Apollinaire

Private collection

5
The Disquieting Muses

De Chirico might have been seriously ill with influenza in the autumn of 1918, but he was not too ill to mourn the loss of Apollinaire, his first perceptive and helpful friend in Paris when he had arrived there from Italy in 1911. Apollinaire had never lost faith in him, and twice in the last few months of his life he had mentioned him favourably in reviews, saying that he had never been influenced by any French painter and was now beginning to influence young painters in Italy. He also mentioned that Carrà, the 'old futurist' (not the 'former futurist'), was now in tune with the younger man's ideas.

De Chirico knew how much he owed Apollinaire, and if in 1945 he was to sound somewhat offhand about the poet's Saturday gatherings he seems to have been deeply moved by his death in November 1918, just as the armistice was being signed. In December he wrote in the Rome review *Ars Nova* that people who had not known Apollinaire were mistaken in thinking he was a self-satisfied dilettante. 'Instead he was a man crushed . . . [by] universal melancholy' – the painter was still drawn to melancholy – and de Chirico referred to all the sadness of the poet's life, including his imprisonment for the suspected thefts from the Louvre. De Chirico obviously appreciated Apollinaire's early attitude towards him and other struggling young artists: 'He defended the latest painting with disinterested intelligence . . . He was the enemy of all mean tricks and all pettiness in art' and any criticism was expressed with 'refined diplomacy'. He was ready to write for the Italian review *La Voce*, even if he preferred to write in French. The piece ended with a moving evocation of the house at

202 *bis* boulevard Saint-Germain where Apollinaire had lived on the top floor. De Chirico saw it again as though in a dream:

> between the tragic innocence of the vanished canvases by the douanier-painter and the metaphysical buildings by the undersigned I see the light of an oil lamp, cheap clay pipes yellow with nicotine, a long bookcase . . . friends sitting silently in the shadow . . . and then, as though in the luminous beam from a magic lantern there appears on the wall the fateful rectangle of a Veronese sky and against that sky is once again the curving profile of a melancholy centurion . . . It is Apollinaire, Apollinaire the ghost returning, it is the poet friend who supported me in a foreign country and whom I shall never see again.

De mortuis nil nisi bonum: although de Chirico did not forget to talk about himself and his work, this article shows, as do the paintings of the late war years, that if he himself was still something of an enigma, if his voice was still 'speaking darkly', that voice was growing warmer, more human.

Apollinaire had been an innovator who looked constantly into the future, but he now belonged to the past. De Chirico, escaping from the war, was beginning to live in the present, aware of Apollinaire's legacy, *l'esprit nouveau* in art and writing. Even before he officially left the army and Ferrara late in 1918 he was fully occupied with writing, both creative and critical, in addition to painting.

Although the cloud of war had still hung over Europe in early 1918 there had been no shortage of activity in the artistic field. In May of that year de Chirico contributed for the first time to an exhibition in Italy, held at the gallery of the magazine *L'Epoca* in Rome, in the via del Tritone, and moving later to Viareggio. It was an 'independent' exhibition arranged on behalf of the Red Cross and included painters in various styles, such as Carlo Carrà, Ardengo Soffici and other less remembered Italian names. De Chirico did not fare well at the hands of the critics. In *L'Idea Nazionale* of 28 May C.E. Oppo referred to him as a 'tragic metaphysical puppeteer', working in dark, frightening colours, adding 'emerald green skies, vast empty squares, black and white houses' and a sun that had grown dark from universal judgement on things. It was perhaps too soon for de Chirico's six paintings on show to be better appreciated, for anyone apart from the most enlightened critics to understand the true value of *Hector and Andromache* seen as mannequins or the melancholy solitary figure of *The Troubadour* or *The Grand Metaphysician* and the ghostly *The Return*. This last work appears to show the 'return' of the male figure with closed eyes from *The Child's Brain* – perhaps an unconscious, or maybe even half-conscious, memory of de Chirico's father – while at the same time it seems to introduce in reverse the theme of the Prodigal Son – in reverse for it could be said that the artist had visualized the father returning to the son, here shown as a dummy figure, and not the other way round, as described originally by Saint Luke.

De Chirico's work was now to be reintroduced in Paris, for Paul Guillaume, who was still acting as his agent, presented some of his metaphysical paintings at the Vieux Colombier theatre during the interval of a Dada show in November. In the following month he reopened his gallery, now refurbished, in the rue du Faubourg Saint-Honoré, showing work by de Chirico in the excellent company of Matisse, Derain, Picasso and Modigliani.

In fact de Chirico could not complain that the war years had interrupted his career; he had been able to go on working, his paintings had intrigued people, and if his sales were not great, if critics failed to understand him, at least he had work to show – unlike Carrà, who was now painting very little and going through an intellectual crisis. Indeed, in February 1919 de Chirico was able to hold his first one-man show, at the Galleria Bragaglia in Rome, exhibiting several works he had completed in Ferrara. It was not a great success and the only painting sold was a portrait of a girl, seeming to prove that Italian buyers were 'disquieted' by these works and did not want to see them on the walls of their houses. Yet the show occasioned two incidents which the painter never forgot: his first encounter with one Diana Karenne, an actress, who could not think of anything to say except 'What a lot of work', and his first crushing review – a *stroncatura*, to use the word invented by that destructive writer Giovanni Papini.

De Chirico had known Papini much earlier, in Florence, and from now on he assumed that his former friend had organized a dirty-tricks campaign against him. Papini had advised de Chirico to talk to the critic Roberto Longhi and explain the background to his work. The painter did so, 'like a poor innocent', and talked freely about his hopes, his dreams, 'told everything, confessed everything innocently and ingenuously' – only to be rewarded, on 22 February in *Il Tempo*, 'in a perfidious, devilish and horrifying way', with a 'treacherous blow'. The piece, entitled 'To the orthopaedic god', poured scorn and ridicule over the mannequin figures, comparing them to 'legless cripples'. Mention was also made of unmentionable painters, such as the Dutch-born Alma-Tadema, the successful sentimental painter of Victorian England. De Chirico never forgave either Papini or Longhi, asserting that the latter avoided him in the street and only bought a picture from him later in order to give it away. The *stroncatura* obviously hurt de Chirico deeply; it was another of many incidents which gradually drove him into a state of paranoia, and he set about growing a thicker skin.

That same year, 1919, was to bring other important developments for him, but it is vital to remember at this stage how de Chirico the writer had developed during the last few years. In the earliest of his prose writing known to us, the pages written in Paris in 1913 or so and kept among the papers of Paul Eluard and Jean Paulhan, the young painter had written with near-poetic exuberance an enthusiastic evocation of what painting should express and what it should mean to him. During the same year he translated (apparently from a French version) four poems by Schopenhauer and signed his copy of the philosopher's essay 'On Appearances', adding a few words in Latin and giving his name as 'Giorgius de Chirico Florentinus', followed by the date in Roman numerals: 'A.D. MCMXIII'. He seems to have added his translations of the poems at the end of the book. Poems of his own written in Paris around this time were published in Rome in 1980 by the critic Maurizio Fagiolo dell'Arco, who has discovered many important pieces, prose and poetry written by the painter when he was young. One of these short poems was quoted in Chapter 4 because its date was relevant, but other, more lyrical, poems were to follow. The prose fragment he dedicated to Carrà during 1917, 'Viaggio e villeggiatura', has a near-surrealist atmosphere:

> I am sleeping. In my imagination I see shadowy trees by the entrance to a house where I had lived since I was a child. Someone called me from the other room. The motor-boat went swiftly past the promontory. It was afternoon, friends. The sea foamed. A metaphysician in a rose-coloured jersey was sleeping beneath a pine tree. Birds made of coloured tinware moved along the beach.

Another intriguing piece, written during the same year, is 'Promontorio', where the poet-painter describes himself looking at his work from 'the promontory of my twenty-ninth year' and conjures up mysterious visions of 'unplumbed oceans', returning to a theme from Greek mythology that he had used earlier and was to use again later, adapting it whenever he thought it necessary: 'The vessel of the Argonauts has vanished in the ice and snow.' He used this myth in different ways: he likened himself and his fellow artists to explorers searching for a new and valid style of painting, and he often thought of himself as an exile in a foreign land. His home country was the Greece of ancient gods, and one reason why he always hated travel was surely his knowledge that no amount of travelling would ever take him back to that land of true heroes, the ones who remained important to him all his life. He also used poetic prose to make a plea for the formation of a group or a metaphysical school – he wrote about putting up a sign indicating that he was the only shareholder.

He was now working closely with Mario Broglio, who, in addition to 'On Metaphysical Art' and 'Zeuxis the Explorer' already mentioned, published four other important pieces by de Chirico in his journal *Valori Plastici*. They are essential reading for anyone who wants to study the painter's message, and since the review soon became known in most European countries his writing surely reached those at whom it was aimed.

De Chirico also contributed sixteen articles to *Il Convegno*, a review published in Rome and Milan. In 1920 and 1921 these included the pieces about Böcklin and Klinger already quoted, while he also wrote about painters much better known – Raphael, Renoir (whose portraits were to influence him)and Gauguin – and about artists well known at least in Italy at the time: Gaetano Previati and Ardengo Soffici. For *Il Convegno* in August 1920 de Chirico reviewed Carrà's book *Pittura metafisica*, which had been published by Vallecchi in Florence. It might have been a moment for him to take revenge, but he did not condemn the book out of hand. However, he made one telling comment: 'The undersigned has also searched . . . for his own name . . . but to no avail!'

Later written work included a short piece about another metaphysical painter, Giorgio Morandi, which he contributed to the catalogue of the big exhibition *La Fiorentina primaverile* in 1922. Morandi, who has since attained classic status, rarely left his native Bologna but was known to admire de Chirico's work. Just as he limited his travel, Morandi limited his subject matter, preferring bottles and other everyday objects which through his treatment became in fact truly metaphysical – real and unreal at the same time. An important essay by de Chirico on Gustave Courbet was published in the *Rivista di Firenze* in November 1924.

But that is to anticipate, for it was a new, later, de Chirico who took an interest in the nineteenth-century French realist. His own 'realism' for the time being was that of technique. During the none too successful show at the Galleria Bragaglia he had passed a good deal of time in museums and galleries, especially the Villa Borghese, for he had been

> deeply impressed both by the paintings housed there and by the classical beauty of the trees and plants growing round the Villa. It was one morning at the Villa Borghese, in front of a painting by Titian, that I had a revelation of what great painting was: I saw tongues of fire appear in the gallery, while outside, beneath the clear sky over the city, rang out a solemn clangour as of weapons beaten in salute, and together with a great cry of righteous spirits there echoed the sound of a trumpet heralding a resurrection.

It sounds like a religious conversion, and in one way it was, for he thought he was now looking at paintings in a new way: he no longer saw them as 'painted images' – although it is not clear what precisely he did see – and the man who had achieved the individual style of metaphysical painting now spent a great deal of time studying the great works of the past.

Did that vision, that conversion, come at a convenient moment? Did the painter sense that his achievements in Ferrara, and also in Paris earlier, could not be continued for ever at the same pitch, that some change of mood and style was inevitable? Probably. And probably too those 'tongues of fire' provided a useful theatrical device, an impressive explanation for what was a brave decision. Just when he was becoming internationally known he felt bound to announce, first of all to himself, that he was changing course. Was this a way of admitting failure in his search for metaphysical truth? A careful look at his paintings even during the Ferrara period shows that, despite his efforts, a faintly human and sexual element had crept into his work, seeming to prove that transforming people into mannequins had not finally reduced them to abstractions. The people wanted to be alive; they did not want their images to represent ideas only.

Only painters and picture restorers are likely to be closely interested in the experiments which de Chirico now carried out with grinding colours and, on the advice of Nikolai Locoff, a Russian painter and restorer, with working in tempera. Locoff was a skilled copyist, and de Chirico himself, sometimes in Rome, sometimes in Florence, worked hard at making copies of the old masters. Fortunately, however, despite his copying and researching, he also continued to paint original works, some of them recalling the early paintings of his first stay in Florence. But the great metaphysical paintings were 'a procession no one could follow after': he had reached the end of that period, although he was to deny the fact until the end of his life. In fact his most intriguing work in the immediate post-war years was autobiographical, namely several striking self-portraits and at least two double portraits, the subjects being himself and his constant companion during the early days in Rome, his mother.

When they had returned to Rome together from Ferrara after his recovery from Spanish flu, de Chirico and his mother had found a very crowded city and there was nowhere to live. He also had another problem: he had no money at all – not even corporal's pay now – and his mother too was badly off, for the Greek railroad shares she had inherited had lost nearly all their value. However, she succeeded in finding a room in the Park Hotel in the via Lucullo, described by Luisa Spagnoli as 'a second-rate establishment much frequented by artists'. Her son, however, failed to find any helpful friend who might give him some space, and for a time he shared his mother's room, sleeping on a mattress on the floor. His brother was not far away, and the story goes that some time later the two men shared a blue suit; unfortunately for Giorgio he was the taller of the two, and the sleeves came down only to his elbows. However, he now wore his old army cape, which he had had dyed black. During the worst of the winter cold he would borrow a bodice or camisole from his mother and wear it under his shirt.

His mother was useful, and in Rome she made an impression on the neighbours at least, for as soon as she could she left the Park Hotel for furnished rooms, changing them every two weeks or so and arranging to remove her possessions by carriage. Everything was packed in baskets and suitcases, strapped alongside her valuable Turkish carpets, the whole surmounted with another piece of equipment from which she was never parted, a bidet. An elderly woman painter remembered this performance clearly, several decades later, and never forgot the Baronessa's jewellery, which included a fine cross set with brilliants.

De Chirico painted his mother on several occasions but never more strikingly than in the two double portraits of 1919 and 1921. She, understandably, is shown in the foreground on each occasion, looking to the front in the former, to the side in the latter but dominating the scene in both, just as she clearly dominated her son. In the earlier portrait he is shown in profile, but since his hand conceals his mouth and chin he is not obviously recognizable, while in the later work he looks outward with an expression of romantic melancholy, as though asking, 'What can be done about this situation?' or 'What can be done about me?' He seems to accept both questions as inevitable and embellishes the painting with two flowers and two figs. In the earlier work the two figures are separated by two pears; he had used two pear halves in a drawing of 1917, *Autumnal Geometry*.

The inclusion of figs has sent critics to a passage in the painter's novel *Hebdomeros* where he refers to figs as 'immoral', their consumption with cracked ice at breakfast earning 'a punishment of ten or fifteen years' imprisonment'. Was this some childhood memory, some fantasy or a reference to images he had seen in classical paintings while haunting museums and galleries during his copying work? This kind of association remains one of the many de Chirico enigmas, but it illustrates the fascination of the dual-media imagery which occurs constantly in the work of this artist-writer.

He also painted his mother on her own in a conventional manner, while Savinio is said to have painted her too, in his fashion, choosing to show her wearing a ball dress, carrying flowers, while for her face and head he substituted the head of a fierce bird. This, *The Faithful Spouse* of 1929, was Savinio's far from straightforward way of showing his love, just as he had described his father as being cruel to the dog Trollolò. The two sons loved their mother, and she loved them in her nineteenth-century overprotective manner. The brothers, the former 'Dioscuri', were still good friends, and de Chirico painted a double portrait of them too. The surviving family today find it unnecessary to talk about the older generation, but surely the paintings and the writing tell all that we need to know about the relationships between these intriguing people.

De Chirico made no comment about his mother in his *Memoirs* until she died, in 1936, while he was away in the USA. Indeed, in the first seven chapters of the *Memoirs*, which cover the period from his childhood to the end of 1918, he mentioned just two women by name and then only *en passant*: in Chapter 6 he included Marie Laurencin in a list of people whom he saw at Apollinaire's gatherings, and a few pages later he included the novelist Matilde Serao, mainly associated with Naples, in a list of writers who happened to have been born in Greece. In the next chapter he expressed gratitude to the wife of the poet Govoni, but she remains merely 'the Signora'. During the early

Rome period he said he was 'excited' then disappointed by the actress Diana Karenne when she came to the Bragaglia show in 1919. In Chapter 9 he referred to the 'charming Pasqualina', wife of the painter Armando Spadini, but by the end of the same paragraph he was already extolling the articles written by Isabella Far, who had become his second wife by the time he wrote these memoirs. In Chapter 10 he mentioned three sisters called Braun, who were Dalcroze dancers. Then on the next page he suddenly began to generalize in a disparaging way about women, making only one exception in a grudging reference to the young Russian Marie Bashkirtseff, 'who began by being a very beautiful girl, then she wrote very well and painted moderately well; she knew Greek and Latin, was not affected to the point of hysteria but had a touch of it, sometimes busied herself with boring other people, but not always'. He did not add that she died at twenty-four but went straight on to attack the Baronne Hélène d'Oettingen, whom he had known in Paris and who had written, at too great length, in *Les Soirées de Paris*, using the name Roch Grey, as well as painting badly and writing bad novels.

By the time he wrote his *Memoirs* de Chirico seemed to assume that by some obscure process of social change women could only deteriorate; men should be glad, he wrote, that they were born at that time and not later. Nevertheless, he had already made it clear, when talking of the young men who surrounded the poet Vincenzo Cardarelli, founder of the review *La Ronda*, that he was 'proud of the fact that I have never given rise to wild passions in young men and I have never been in love with a Maestro'. Then he found it necessary to make a clear statement of his heterosexuality: 'In any case I would have been in love with a Maestra.' Perhaps he was suddenly aware that the absence of any feminine element in the metaphysical work might cause people to assume he was homosexual.

What did he know about love? He had been strongly attracted to a prostitute in Paris, but his views about women were surely influenced by Schopenhauer, Nietzsche and Weininger. Their message was simple: women did not think; they had no imagination; they were incapable of friendship; they were to be used for the basic purpose of sex. During the successful days of futurism two women had defied such attitudes. One of them, Valentine de Saint-Point, said to be a granddaughter of Victor Hugo, had published in 1913 a leaflet entitled *Futurist Manifesto for Lust*; her radical views were attacked in *Lacerba*, even though it supported futurism. The other was the beautiful and fascinating Marchesa Casati, who impressed the futurists and was painted by Giacomo Balla, one of their number. But Boccioni, that other futurist, preferred to paint his mother rather than any other model of any age.

As de Chirico worked hard at his copying and research into technique, he lost no time in urging other painters to follow his example, publishing his article 'The Return to the Craft' in *Valori Plastici* in 1920. He told painters they must learn to draw, quoting Ingres's observation that a painting based on good drawing is always likely to be fairly well painted. He urged his readers to study statues, 'to dehumanize you a little', and if it was not possible to study them in museums then the students should buy plaster copies and work from them. They would have to work hard, and in his last sentence he wrote in a self-satisfied way, 'As for me, I am calm, and I adorn myself with three words that I wish to be the seal of all my work: *Pictor classicus sum*.'

He was asserting a new complacency, but had he truly embarked on a new phase of creativity? He still painted a few works that could be described as metaphysical, but today they seem too crowded and fragmented. The 'Roman Villa' series, where the houses are surmounted by statues, are decorative in their way and maintain de Chirico's links with the classical world, but his admirers tend to lose interest when confronted by a goddess sitting on a cloud. Various echoes of Böcklin appear, but the five or six years following de Chirico's return to Rome offer fascinating biographical evidence of another kind – the series of portraits and especially the self-portraits.

Despite the negative attitude he had displayed towards women, he certainly painted them – all types of women, including peasants in costume, anonymous sitters and a striking portrait (1922) of Amelia Bontempelli, wife of the author Massimo Bontempelli. Her novels, which she signed 'Diotima', are surely unread today, but de Chirico may well have been flattered by her husband's book *La Scacchiera davanti allo Specchio* (*The Chessboard in Front of the Mirror*), for it was influenced by his metaphysical painting and the writer used the phrase 'magical realism', adopted in Germany to describe the work carried out by artists there who had been influenced by de Chirico.

The self-portraits are particularly intriguing, for there are so many of them that one feels de Chirico must have been searching for his true image. Also, he did not always seem ready to appear on his own: he felt he must add a classical bust, of Mercury or Euripides, or even show his own head twice over – once realistically, once as a kind of marble silhouette. Was he living in ancient Greece or in the real world of Rome, Florence, Milan? There is one interesting development: the painted figure no longer holds a notice, as appeared in earlier self-portraits, reading, for instance, 'NULLA SINE TRAGŒDIA GLORIA': he begins to use his hands in dramatic gestures, indicating either infinity or some message from the ancient world, while his hair often hangs over his forehead as though he sees himself as a romantic hero still in the mood of mystery and melancholy.

However, if he was forever searching for himself, his work had been found by critics, dealers and buyers in several European countries – Germany, Holland and of course France. The 'revelation' in the Villa Borghese had taken place in 1919 and so, by a coincidence of the post-war situation, had the early formulation of surrealism in Paris. Although it began 'officially' in 1924, with the surrealist manifesto, some historians and participants have quoted earlier dates. It is known that the word was used in 1917 by Apollinaire apropos the ballet *Parade*, while the same year saw the first meeting of André Breton and Jacques Vaché, who was either a living example of surrealism or else a poseur, whose display of cynical disillusioned bravado on the battlefield was guaranteed to attract attention, as he wanted. Vaché died in 1919, either by suicide or by accident, but the same year saw the rise of automatic writing, held by Breton to be a crucial event in the pre-history of the movement. At the same time the poets Philippe Soupault and Paul Eluard discovered de Chirico. The dream-like atmosphere of the early paintings, a mingling of real and unreal, seemed to express everything the surrealists were interested in. In 1922 Breton, presenting an exhibition of de Chirico's work at Paul Guillaume's gallery in March 1922, wrote, 'I think that a true modern mythology is in formation. And it is Giorgio de Chirico who is setting up the record of it for all time.'

Art histories are full of surrealist paintings reflecting the influence of de Chirico, and there are several stories of the dramatic effects his work could have. Magritte said it caused him to see his true vocation; according to a lecture he gave in Antwerp in 1938, he saw in de Chirico's work 'a new vision in which the spectator discovers his solitude once again and hears the silence of the world'. He had not forgotten his discovery nineteen years later, writing that his first sight of the painting *The Song of Love* was 'one of the most disturbing in my whole life: my eyes "saw thought" for the first time'. Yves Tanguy is said to have jumped off a Paris bus in order to take a long look at an early de Chirico painting glimpsed in a gallery window; he afterwards learned that André Breton had first come across de Chirico's work in precisely the same way. The Italian painter was inescapable, but he was in Rome, not Paris, and, if the surrealists read *Valori Plastici*, it took them some time to catch up with 'the return to the craft', although at least one of de Chirico's copies (of a work by Raphael) was included in the March 1922 Paul Guillaume show, along with other post-metaphysical work.

In the meantime surrealism was moving on through the Dada influence of the first series of the magazine *Littérature*, published from March 1919 to August 1921. The magazine's range was wide: the title came from Paul Valéry; its contributors included André Gide, Raymond Radiguet (still only sixteen at the time), a host of forgotten names, and of course Breton and his coterie. In January 1920 Breton wrote about a pamphlet which reproduced twelve of de Chirico's paintings. The second series of the review ran from March 1922 to June 1924, and in the first issue de Chirico made three appearances. There was a reproduction of *The Child's Brain* – owned of course by Breton – a piece about the painter by Roger Vitrac, who went on to publish a short book about him in 1927, and a letter from de Chirico to Breton dated that same month. It was a long letter, and those who read it – mainly surrealists and their supporters, no doubt – must have wondered what was going on. The painter addressed the poet as his 'very dear friend', who had presumably given him some encouragement, for he wrote that 'For a long time I worked without hope.' He said that he had to 'clarify one point . . . the point which has to do with my painting of today.' (The Paul Guillaume exhibition was in progress at the time.) He knew that he was being criticized for producing 'museum art' and that it was being said that he had lost his way, but he had a clear conscience and was 'full of inner joy'. He was certain that eventually the value of his new work would be understood, and surely it was a good sign that he had come to know Breton.

He enlarged on what had changed in the arts generally, although he was not going to talk about 'neo-classicism, revival etc.' He spoke instead about 'this magnificent romanticism which we have created' and said that 'these dreams and visions which troubled us' would be judged by posterity. He mentioned 'Apollinaire and a few others, my paintings, those of Picasso, Derain and a few others' but went on to explain how the problem of *métier*, craft, had 'tormented' him, how he had made copies, ground his own colours, etc. He was convinced that his own painting was now much better. He thought the impressionists had used the wrong methods in their attempts to portray light: 'the source of shadows' was their only palette. He would send Breton a photograph of a recent self-portrait which he thought 'could figure in the Louvre'. Although de Chirico sounded tolerably well pleased with himself, he apologized for his 'barbarian' French. He told Breton that he embraced him.

Breton does not seem to have answered the letter: his reply was its publication in *Littérature*.

Relations with Breton were not easy, however, for de Chirico apparently promised four sketches for inclusion in Breton's book of poems *Clair de terre* (1923), but they never came and the book appeared with a portrait of the poet by Picasso. But relationships with the surrealists did not break down at once. In 1922 Max Ernst produced that intriguing work *Le Rendezvous des Amis*, eighteen of them, all numbered, with a key below. De Chirico can be seen in the back row, but he is not actually present, for Ernst shows him as a bust (not in any way *ressemblant*) standing on a classical fluted pillar. The column may be intended to evoke de Chirico's origin, his painting or, since he was still in Rome, his absence from Paris. To his right, slightly in front, stands Breton – shown larger than the others and looking as though he had just dashed in – while by de Chirico's left shoulder stands Gala Eluard (later Gala Dalí). The painting is an essential part of the history of surrealism; later on de Chirico attacked the movement and all its practitioners with unparalleled fury – but not yet.

Breton was given to displays of great enthusiasm, but they did not always last long. He was a born authoritarian, which explains why his leadership of the surrealists was never questioned, and he did not like to be proved wrong. How dare de Chirico change his style – for that is what had happened – without his permission? The painter had meant a great deal to the early or proto-surrealists, and Breton had helped him by advising the wealthy but cautious collector Jacques Doucet to buy his work. What were the surrealists to think of him now? Breton had not forgiven Jacques Vaché for dying, for deserting him; he would not tolerate another desertion. And maybe a rumour had already reached him that the painter did not copy only Raphael and other classical painters: he also copied himself.

Strong evidence of this came from Rome in 1924. De Chirico was convinced that André Breton had ordered his supporters to boycott all his later work, but that did not prevent Paul Eluard and his wife from coming to Rome, buying a self-portrait by de Chirico exhibited at the Biennale which opened there in October 1923 and then visiting the painter in his studio, where he painted a portrait of them together. Gala Eluard wanted to buy *The Disquieting Muses*, that important painting from the Ferrara days, owned at the time by the painter's friend and admirer in Florence Dr Giorgio Castelfranco. They also wanted to buy from Mario Broglio the equally famous *Sacred Fish*. Unfortunately the owners did not want to sell for the prices offered, despite the painter's 'insistence'. So he made a different kind of offer: 'If you would like exact copies of these two paintings,' he wrote to the

Eluards, 'I can do them for you at 1,000 lire each. The only drawbacks to these copies will be their execution with better materials and with greater technical understanding.' This was apparently written on 10 March 1924 and has been described as the first evidence, direct from de Chirico himself, of his activities as a self-copyist. James Thrall Soby reports that Eluard commissioned a copy of *The Disquieting Muses*. In June de Chirico said that he had had no news of Breton for a long time and hoped he was not angry with him about the *Disquieting Muses* affair. But he surely was.

De Chirico was still developing that deprecatory attitude to everyone and everything that continued to grow blacker for the rest of his life. In the 1923 Rome Biennale he had exhibited some of the 'Roman Villa' series. He thought his contribution was very good – as were his sales, mainly to foreigners – but the critical response was poor. This led him to become inversely rhapsodic in describing it – especially the review by the well-known Emilio Cecchi, which de Chirico described as 'failure to understand, confusion, bad faith and envy, blended together in a symphony of such beauty that if it could have been translated into music it would have figured worthily in . . . those concerts which in Rome today are called *musica viva* but which ought to be called still-born music'. What in fact had Cecchi written? He maintained that the effect of the paintings was not 'entirely negative' but said it was debatable whether de Chirico was really a painter in the full sense of the term. He was a 'fantasist, a visionary, an individual; and for better or worse, an artist'. And Cecchi added that de Chirico's feeling for the hideous and his vulgar expedients 'could not succeed in depriving all his things of a sinister fascination, between the legendary and the provincial'.

De Chirico fared no better when he showed at the Venice Biennale of 1924: his work was found to be 'heavy' and 'illogical'. However, during this year there occurred two events which could be described as 'logical', for his painting and his solitary life meant they were bound to happen: for the first time he was invited to work in the theatre, first in Paris; then, when visiting another theatre, in Rome, he fell in love. There had been a theatrical element in his work at different periods –

unexpectedly perhaps in early works such as *The Enigma of the Oracle* of 1910 and then undeniably in the *Hector and Andromache* subjects painted in Ferrara. In addition he had been dramatizing himself in portraits during the last few years. As for love, painting was infinitely more important to him than anything else, but so far his only muse of the conventionally feminine kind had been supplied by the marble or plaster bust of Venus or some other deity. He was now in his thirties – thirty-six in 1924 – and, although disappointed that his current painting was not better understood and appreciated, was well known for his earlier work. His celebrity and the theatrical effect of the self-portraits, the atmosphere of mystery, melancholy and enigma, were inevitably attractive to women.

6
Salve Lutetia

THE year 1924 brought developments that were not only emotional but also polemical. This was a crucial year in the development of surrealism, for Breton's first *Manifesto of Surrealism* was published after *Littérature* came to an end with the June issue (the thirteenth), and the review *La Révolution surréaliste* first appeared on 1 December. The manifesto was described by the surrealist historian Patrick Waldberg in 1965 as 'a fervent and haughty little book', and so it is, but it is still essential reading, along with the second manifesto, of 1929 and Breton's *Surrealism and Painting* of 1928.

Nearly halfway through the first manifesto Breton defines 'once and for all' what the word 'surrealism' means, at least to him and his group: it is 'Pure psychic automatism through which it is intended to express, either verbally, or in writing, or by any other means, the true functioning of thought, dictated by thought in the absence of all control exercised by reason, outside all aesthetic or moral preoccupation.' He goes on to give a definition of surrealism as a philosophical term: it is 'based on the belief in the superior reality of certain forms of association previously neglected, the all-powerful nature of dream, the disinterested play of thought'. With these definitions in mind, it is easy to see why de Chirico's early work was so useful to the surrealists: it seemed to express everything they believed in, and it had done so in advance, created by a young man no one had heard of, working alone until discovered by Picasso and Apollinaire.

Despite Breton's unease concerning the new trends in the painter's work and de Chirico's long letter about his new general approach to painting, the surrealists and their supporters still admired the metaphysical work, which they could see fairly easily in small galleries and shows and more easily still on the walls of each other's apartments. Some of de Chirico's drawings were displayed at the Bureau of Surrealist Research at 15 rue de Grenelle, an ambitious venture which aimed at first to collect useful material from members of the public. Surrealism had taken over the avant-garde scene. Dada, for example, was no longer in favour – it seemed to lead nowhere, and the surrealists were determined to get somewhere, with their own type of revolution, the 'revolution of the mind', leading ultimately to the revolution of society.

In a way that was unexpected, especially to himself, de Chirico was omnipresent. He had been present in *Le Rendezvous des Amis* in 1922 only as a bust surmounting a classical column; now he figured in two photographs (by Man Ray) on the front cover of the first issue of *La Révolution surréaliste*. He was shown standing in the middle of the back row among a group of a dozen or so surrealists attending a session of automatic writing, performed, if that is the word, by Robert Desnos dictating to Breton's first wife, Simone. In another photograph, occupying the right of the cover, virtually all those present at the same session look downward at Desnos, Simone Breton and her typewriter. Only de Chirico, still in the back row, is looking straight at the camera. The painter stands with his head slightly to one side. Was he not interested in automatic writing, such a crucial element in early surrealism? His own imaginative writing is rich with the unconscious association of images, like his painting, but it is a long way from automatism, for if it is often emotional it is also highly wrought and sometimes 'literary' in the traditional sense. Was he ensuring that the camera would produce one more portrait – one that he had not painted himself? He seemed anxious to assert himself.

On the wall behind Breton, who stands two positions to the painter's right, hangs *The Dream of Tobias*, an enigmatic work of 1917, which includes at least one reference – the fish – to the story told in the Book of Tobit of the biblical Apocrypha. The tall central panel has been described as a 'thermometer–barometer–metronome', while the word AIDEL, spelled out vertically along it, has been thought to have a double significance: a memory of de Chirico's elder sister Adèle, who died in infancy, and a link with the Greek word for mystery and obscurity. There is no dream in the tale of Tobias and Tobit. This is not as much of a digression as it might seem, for paradoxically the painter, who was in many ways forward-looking, was continually preoccupied with ancient Greece and also with the modern Greece of his early memories.

The first issue of *La Révolution surréaliste* was much concerned with dreams and automatic writing; it contained drawings by de Chirico, Max Ernst and others whose work is remembered only by specialists, but more importantly it contained descriptions of dreams by Breton and by de Chirico, the latter's being given pride of place. It is a strikingly autobiographical document: 'In vain I struggle with the man whose eyes are louche and very gentle. Each time I take hold of him he frees himself gently by holding out his arms and these arms possess an unknown strength, an incalculable power . . .' The dreamer sees again 'a square of great metaphysical beauty; perhaps it is the piazza Cavour in Florence, or perhaps one of those very beautiful squares in Turin, or perhaps neither the one nor the other . . .' He then sees his father in a pâtisserie (de Chirico had painted biscuits and desserts); he contemplates running away; he is afraid his father is in danger; he feels that if he enters the pâtisserie he will need a dagger – then the crowd sweeps him away; he feels his father is like a thief on the run, 'and I awoke in the anguish of this thought'. It was something of a literary dream: it looked back over the painter's past, while the style anticipated the writing to be found in *Hebdomeros*, his novel of 1929, and other prose pieces.

The surrealists still continued to believe in de Chirico, otherwise the next six numbers of *La Révolution surréaliste* would presumably not have included reproductions of his work. Number 4 also included 'Two declarations on art' by him, while Number 5, on 15 October 1925, carried his poem 'Une nuit', dated 1911–13, written during his early days in Paris and again about a dream. Some of the imagery seems to refer directly to his paintings – the cardboard rocks seem to come from a Böcklin-style landscape – but some images are foreign to the work already known: the line 'Around the table the women were reading' seems to foreshadow the work of the surrealist painter Paul Delvaux, which of course came later, while one image seems to have a homosexual connotation not to be found at least in any obvious way in de Chirico's visual work:

> Everywhere was meditation
> And the monk passed by me once more. Through the holes in his rotting hair-shirt I saw the beauty of his body, pale and white like a statue of love.
> When I awoke happiness was still asleep beside me.

One is reminded of the painter's description of himself a few years earlier in Rome, when he realized, after talking freely to Roberto Longhi, that he had been 'a poor innocent'; he always considered Freudian analysis to be a waste of time. He also condemned homosexuality but never mentioned that his painter friend Filippo de Pisis, from Ferrara, was of this inclination.

However, during the autumn and winter of 1924 de Chirico was not merely a name and a photograph in *La Révolution surréaliste*. At the request of Erik Satie, the Italian composer Alfredo Casella, who had studied in Paris and was now in mid-career, had composed the music for a ballet, *La Jarre*, based on a short story, 'La Giara', by Luigi Pirandello. Casella already knew the two de Chirico brothers, and Giorgio was invited to design the sets and costumes for this story of peasant life, which was to be performed by the Ballets Suédois of Rolf de Maré, with choreography by Jean Börlin, at the Théâtre des Champs-Elysées. The sketches for the twelve costumes, preserved in the Swedish Museum of the Dance, seem to have been conventional enough, while the sets included buildings typical of de Chirico's earlier work, before he began to include destabilized planes. In 1913 he had been told by Dunoyer de Segonzac and Luc-Albert Moreau, the selectors for the Salon des Indépendants, that he would make a good stage designer, for his work was found to be very 'decorative' and scenographic. At the time he had assumed that this faint praise merely proved the failure of the two artists to understand his work, but the Ferrara paintings alone show how, in spite of himself perhaps, he had adopted a form of dramatic presentation, while his figures seem to be on stage. Later in life he was ready to accept many commissions for the stage sets and costumes for ballet and opera.

Meanwhile the programme for what was to turn out to be the last Ballets Suédois season was designed by Francis Picabia, who came close to Dada and surrealism without ever identifying with any group. De Chirico's portraits of Casella and Pirandello were included, in addition to one of his self-portraits. When asked for his ideas about the ballet in general, de Chirico said what he thought: the ballet needed to rid itself of 'a certain aestheticism' and incorporate new elements. He believed that in this way the ballet, like the cinema, could replace the prose and operatic theatre, 'which is slowly disappearing'. A controversial statement, indeed, but he added that 'these are not things to write in a programme'.

Other theatres, other programmes. It was probably after visiting Paris for *La Jarre* that he wrote a prose piece 'Vale Lutetia' ('Farewell to Paris'), published first in the *Rivista di Firenze* of February 1925 and reprinted, entitled '*Salve Lutetia*' ('Greetings to Paris'), in Léonce Rosenberg's *Bulletin de l'effort moderne* in Paris in March 1927. In it he recalled how he found the city and all the posters on the hoardings to be 'metaphysical'. Nevertheless he was soon back in Rome, living with his mother and brother at via Apennino 25b.

By the beginning of 1925 the two men, if remaining too poor to buy themselves respectable clothes, could nevertheless enjoy the social activities organized by a few well-off, hospitable people interested in the arts. Among such people were the Signorellis, whom de Chirico had known during the war. They were both doctors, bought paintings, and ran a kind of salon to which painters, writers and theatrical figures were regularly invited. The two de Chirico brothers came with their mother, who as usual wore her splendid jewellery, listened to the conversation but did not join in. However, she impressed the young Signorelli daughter, possibly through the theatrical quality of her presence.

Olga Signorelli was Russian-born, and it may have been in her house that a young Russian dancer first saw Giorgio de Chirico. Late in life, during the 1970s, Raissa Gurievitch Krol could not remember exactly where she met him first – possibly at the Signorellis, she thought – but she certainly saw more of him through the Teatrino degli Undici, a small avant-garde theatre group founded early in 1925 by Pirandello and named after the eleven people, mainly writers, including Massimo Bontempelli, but with at least one actor, who had helped him to start the project. The season opened on 2 April, and on the 28th came a performance of Stravinsky's *The Soldier's Tale* (1918), based on a libretto adapted by the Swiss writer C.-F. Ramuz from a Russian story. The text had been translated into Italian by Savinio, who was closely involved with other productions, including his own one-act *tragedia mimica La Morte di Niobe*, for which he had composed the music and his brother Giorgio had designed the decor.

The performances took place in the Palazzo Odaleschi, which Pirandello had refurbished. He attempted to exercise strict control over his performers, who were mostly, but not exclusively, young. He would point to his hat and tell everyone, 'If any *storia sentimentale* begins here I shall pick up this hat and you will never see me again.' In other words, no love affairs. But Pirandello himself, whose wife suffered from an incurable mental illness, had fallen passionately in love with a girl called Marta Abba, apparently a good actress. However, no intimate relationship could develop, for Pirandello knew very well that the young, virginal, well-brought-up Marta was destined to find a suitable Catholic husband and settle down. Pirandello's attempt to ban other budding love affairs was a notable failure, too, for both the de Chirico brothers found wives in this theatrical entourage. Savinio chose Maria Morino, who was already experienced as an actress and had known the world-famous Eleonora Duse, while it might be said of Giorgio that Raissa Gurievitch Krol chose him.

In 1924 Raissa was thirty-four and de Chirico was thirty-six. She came of a rich family: her Ukrainian father had owned vast territories in Poland and Finland and also had business interests in Berlin. Along with an Italian lawyer, Riccardo Gualino (one of the early collectors of modern art), he had planned a big drainage operation in St Petersburg, but when the Revolution forced him to give up the enterprise he took refuge in Finland, living with his family (plus ten servants and a resident hairdresser and dressmaker) in a splendid villa originally furnished for Tsar Nicholas, who had often brought his ailing young son here for convalescence and rest. Raissa had not seen a great deal of Russia, but she had trained for the ballet and, along with her brothers and sisters, moved in a highly cultured environment: the brothers' friends included Maxim Gorky and the great bass Chaliapin. Once, after a ridiculous party during a long holiday in Finland, the young people decorated the vast drawing-room in the villa – formerly the Tsarina's music room – with futurist paintings. They had no worries. One of Raissa's sisters became Princess Obolensky, another married a famous lawyer, while Raissa married George Gurievitch Krol, a theatrical director. They had met while studying for the stage in Moscow with the well-known Russian actor and director Vsevold Emilievitch Meyerhold, who had worked with Stanislavsky for a time when he was young.

A few years before she died Raissa said that de Chirico had experienced the *coup de foudre*, love at first sight, for her. Old photographs of her show a direct, outgoing expression, a high rounded forehead, a mouth that looks always ready to smile. One theatrical picture reveals her in a defiant pose, her eyes – always described as intensely blue – ready to challenge anyone who disturbed her. De Chirico was probably attracted to her liveliness, and she had to confess to her husband that she had fallen in love too, with an unsuccessful painter called Giorgio de Chirico. George Krol was deeply upset; he burst into tears and uttered a warning: 'Raissa, be very careful. Don't trust an Italian.' But she did, and the rejected Krol returned to Russia, where he later drowned in mysterious circumstances. Accident or suicide? Raissa did not know. Nobody ever knew.

Why was she attracted to de Chirico, a controversial and unsuccessful man of thirty-six? 'Because he was shy,' she maintained. He was also awkward, clumsy and untalkative, although he had mastered several languages. He looked carefully at everything; his expression was unusual, interesting: she was convinced he was a genius. He was tall, she remembered; he was very kind. He must also have been possessive: he did not want her to continue dancing or acting. Was he handsome? She was not sure, but at one point, late in life, she described him as 'rather handsome'. One other person who knew de Chirico and his brother during the 1930s remembered neither of them as good-looking, but everyone noticed Giorgio's hair, which hung down over his forehead. Savinio reacted to talk from others, Giorgio did not: he remained *chiuso*, as Dr Boschi of the Villa del Seminario had described him in Ferrara.

Raissa apparently persuaded her new lover that he must go back to Paris. In Rome he was too poor to buy her a cup of coffee, but in Paris his paintings seemed to be selling. Giorgio hated travel, but, just as he was accustomed to doing what his mother told him, he now obeyed Raissa. (He once referred to her unkindly as the 'dominating Slav Jewess'.) He arrived in Paris in the autumn of 1925, having taken the shared clothes with him, leaving his brother *nudo*, according to Raissa.

De Chirico seems to have been very much in love, for back in July 1925 he had written Raissa a letter which she was to keep for years: he mentioned two letters he had received from her – they were 'beautiful and sad', like her, and now they were folded over his heart. She was his 'very pure angel'; he said that he was ready to obey her orders; he was ready to die for her, to give her not only his work, his love, his friendship but his blood: if he had to. He was working hard, he was very inspired – 'my soul that you have purified and exalted exists only for you and for painting'. Her artistic gifts had impressed him more than those of any other woman. He was writing in bed and was now going to read *Tristan and Iseult*. He would write to her every day; he was dedicated to her for ever; he was ready to do anything for her; he would earn well in Paris, and it would all be for her.

Raissa explained later why he found she had 'purified' him. She told a journalist that before he met her 'he had only frequented women of a certain type' and habitually visited 'those houses . . . Do you understand?' she asked. 'In fact,' she went on, 'he hardly saw any difference between sex and love, nor between one woman and another.' This surely explains those many sexless mannequin figures in the pictures from the Ferrara days and the slow change to sexual differentiation in the paintings, which seemed to coincide with his own slow and late maturity.

Raissa quickly joined him in Paris, and as soon as she was divorced they were married, living first in the rue Bonaparte on the Left Bank, where they had a studio, a kitchen and a bathroom.

Giorgio worked hard, and she worked too, in a different way, for she decided to follow a course in archaeology at the Sorbonne. She would go out early every morning and returned to the apartment about eleven o'clock when her husband was just getting up. She said that he liked life to be arranged this way, but she denied that her studies, which filled the place with photographs and drawings of ancient Greek pillars and capitals, had any effect on de Chirico, even though such images were beginning to appear more and more in his work. She maintained that he did not need to be reminded of the ancient world: it was always in his thoughts. Raissa in fact earned academic success with a thesis about the Greek and Roman antiquities which had been preserved at the Château de Versailles and was later to embark on a new career in archaeology.

But what was happening to de Chirico's career? The work he produced at this period seems to show his uncertainty. Where was he going? Paul Guillaume was courageous enough to buy his new work, mainly as a collector, but he did not put it on show. In May 1925 Léonce Rosenberg, who now acted as his agent and dealer, had arranged a one-man show for him and the surrealists had hated it – hated these larger-than-life faceless figures, such as *Souvenir of the Iliad*. André Breton had begun to publish in *La Révolution surréaliste* instalments of his future book *Surrealism and Painting*; in this he dismissed *The Roman Legionary Looking at the Conquered Country* as mediocre and immoral – immoral because it implied old-style colonialism, anathema to the surrealists. The painter's faithful Italian admirer Dr Castelfranco had tried to defend him in his introduction to the catalogue for the Rosenberg show, but he had not convinced the surrealists that the new style had any value. Max Morise, writing in the fourth issue of *La Révolution surréaliste* (July 1925), thought that de Chirico was wasting his time in worrying about technique and decided that his depictions of figures from the ancient world implied a renunciation of the metaphysical work. He was not sure if they forecast some new miracle. The following year the review published a depressing document: a reproduction of a painting of *Orestes and Electra* (shown the previous year by Rosenberg) crossed through with thick black lines, indicating total rejection. The work had been shown in Milan, and de Chirico now seemed to be having more success in Italy, having left it, than he was having in Paris. However, by 1926 he was becoming better known overseas: his work was shown at the Brighton Art Gallery in Britain and at the Brooklyn Museum in New York, and in 1928 he had his first one-man show in the USA, at the Valentine Gallery, also in New York.

De Chirico's writing had attracted attention when *Valori Plastici* was a valued review, and in 1925 Mario Broglio's small publishing firm brought out his booklet on Gustave Courbet, the great French realist. De Chirico wanted to show that 'realism', when skilfully handled, was not so far from the metaphysical as might have appeared. He also wrote an interesting essay ('Statues, Furniture and Generals') for the October 1927 issue of *Le Bulletin de l'effort moderne*. Here de Chirico explained some paintings that might have seemed odd, the 'Furniture in the Valley' series, again autobiographical in origin, for they recall the threat of earthquakes in Volos, when the furniture was often brought outside, and also the endless house moves de Chirico had to endure, when furniture stood on the pavement waiting for removal men. (Savinio's *Tutta la Vita* of 1945 also contained fantasies involving furniture.)

In the meantime de Chirico and Raissa continued to live together, presumably happily, and as the painter gradually became more successful they were able to move to a much grander apartment, in the rue Meissonier in the seventeenth arrondissement, while Giorgio had a separate studio. Raissa was proud of the rue Meissonier apartment and liked to imagine associations with Zola, for Nana had lived in this street, she thought. (Actually, she was not far wrong: Zola described Nana's splendid house as being at the corner of the rue Cardinet where it crossed the avenue de Villiers, very near the rue Meissonier.) She recalled that nobody had come to see them when she and her husband had lived in the rue Bonaparte, but now things were different. During the next few years everyone came: Jean Cocteau, 'Coco' Chanel, the dancer and choreographer Serge Lifar, Diaghilev himself and a young composer who had earlier attracted the great impresario; this was Igor Markevitch, who later wrote in his recollections, *Etre et avoir été*, a few highly amusing lines about the painter and his wife. De Chirico entertained a lot, he said, and walked among his guests like an imposing elephant seal, as though he belonged to a race different from that of the other earthlings. Markevitch added that he was particularly friendly with the painter's wife, 'one of those comfortable plump Russian women whose hospitable breasts can easily be imagined, full of bortsch'. The fair-haired dancer drawn and painted by de Chirico had obviously lost her ballerina's figure, while her husband was no longer the anguished young man who allowed his hair to fall over his forehead; photographs taken during the late 1920s show that his cheeks had filled out.

Why had de Chirico become so successful, given that he and his work had been so badly treated by the surrealist critics? Because, perhaps, these critics were not taken too seriously by older collectors, and because the disruption they caused when the opportunity offered – at the funeral of Anatole France and at a banquet in honour of the symbolist poet Saint-Pol Roux, for example – only gained them enemies. De Chirico may have been hurt by their attitude for a time – they had printed obituary notices of him; they had staged counter-exhibitions in order to annoy him – but he had obviously learned how to cope with their attacks. But the skin that had begun to grow thicker was perhaps not yet thick enough, and it was unfortunate to say the least that one day when André Breton visited his studio he found de Chirico engaged in copying one of his earlier works and later described the incident in *Surrealism and Painting*.

This copying activity (never mentioned in his *Memoirs*, of course) may have helped de Chirico to earn extra money very quickly. According to Raissa – at this stage many statements must be 'according to Raissa', for she was the only one to report events – a good deal of money came from the painter's success as a self-copyist (for which his copies of Raphael and other old masters had given him plenty of practice). It appears that de Chirico and his wife were invited to dinner by the collector Jacques Doucet, who now owned *The Disquieting Muses*, bought on the advice of André Breton. Doucet apparently told the painter how much he would like to have one of the Italian piazza works from 1914. De Chirico replied that he was sure he still had one, but he took care that Raissa would not hear what he said, for she knew very well that all these early works had been sold. Shortly afterwards she was away at San Remo briefly, recovering from an operation, but on her return she learned that her husband had sold a 'piazza' to Doucet, having created a work in his former style and added the date 1914. It so happened that André Breton was away from Paris too, but he found out. Doucet was furious and wanted his money back. The surrealists decided to keep the affair quiet; the money was not returned, but de Chirico was severely scolded. He was not dishonest, Raissa believed; he was like a child: when he wanted something he had to have it, and in this case it was money. It was also, surely, his way of getting back at the surrealists for their insistence that only the metaphysical paintings were important. At the same time he apparently enjoyed playing a trick on Doucet. When Raissa told him on some other occasion that he was doing something 'morally inadmissible', he replied that he was born to be not a moralist but a painter. Raissa was shocked, for she had been brought up very strictly. The strictness practised by de Chirico's father had been of a different kind.

The painter had a valuable assistant, Vladimir Ivanovitch, a former colonel in the White Russian army, who, like so many others with the same background, was now trying to support himself in Paris. Vladimir was supposed to do the cooking, but he was often in trouble because he could only cook potatoes, and de Chirico complained about it. However, he had good manners, charmed the women visitors and apparently helped his employer to paint and copy in very quick time. Many years later Raissa described how they worked. The painter would take a canvas, draw the subject and then, in pencil, divide the area into little squares and write the names of the colours in each square. Vladimir would then paint each square in the colour indicated, the painter would carry out the shading, work on it a little 'and the picture was done'. Raissa added that her husband would occasionally employ other painters, including, for example, Gregorio Sciltian, born in Russia in 1900, who had been trained in Vienna and when later in Paris had been influenced by the cubists. In this way de Chirico was able to produce a vast amount of work very quickly. It all seems hard to believe, but at this period of his life de Chirico had become obsessed with selling. At the same time Raissa remembered that he would occasionally lose his temper and express his rage by breaking the china and glass ornaments in the apartment. The unfortunate Vladimir would then have to try to mend them.

In July 1928 de Chirico was forty. In some ways he might have been reasonably content with his life, at least on a personal level. He and Raissa were living together in a comfortable apartment, happily still, as far as is known. He had, after all, painted *Les Amoureux* (*The Lovers*) in 1926, the title at least seeming to acknowledge that love might exist – something he had been unwilling to admit in the past; although admittedly the 'lovers' of the painting are not attractive, being mannequins with ovoid heads resembling cotton-wool rugby balls. Raissa had presumably learned how to deal with a far from easy husband who was obsessed with unsolvable problems and who felt that nobody understood his painting. Critics might have come to value his early work for artistic, literary and financial reasons, but they persisted in denigrating all his later and current productions. So, by way of revenge, he had cynically decided to copy the early work, using assistants to help him make quick predated versions of paintings in his earlier style to produce material that would sell quickly. He remained totally self-centred, living only for his work, preoccupied with the elements that contributed to it – all of them remembrances of things past.

Raissa maintained that her husband was constantly looking for a woman who would tell him what to do, as his mother had always done, so he probably did not complain when the Baronessa lived with them, as she did for a time, perhaps intermittently. In Rome she had apparently spent her days at Rosati's in the via Veneto, smoking and quietly watching the passers-by. If she chose similar café terraces in Paris, she still needed some more active form of self-expression and found it in having violent quarrels with her son. Raissa had never witnessed such quarrels in her life. One evening the argument had been so fierce – she did not say what it was about, if she even knew, but it was probably money – that she felt convinced that mother and son would not want to remain under the same roof, at least not that night. She slipped out of the apartment, went to a neighbouring hotel and booked a room for her mother-in-law. When she came back she realized she had wasted her time: mother and son were now talking amiably as though nothing had happened. Raissa could hardly believe it. She had been shocked, for in her own puritanical family such scenes had never taken place; she had not learned to understand the Italians or the de Chiricos.

Giorgio had been his mother's favourite as her sons had grown up, for his health had been bad and he had needed her. Now he was financially successful, by whatever methods, and she approved of that. But, like any dominating mother, the Baronessa did not enjoy seeing her sons take an interest in other women. According to Raissa, when the family lived in Rome she had even forbidden Savinio to marry Maria Morino, the actress he had met at the Teatrino degli Undici. But the young couple outwitted her and married in secret in 1926. When the Baronessa found out she would not allow them to share a bedroom in the family apartment, thus perpetuating the ridiculously old-fashioned ideas of her late husband. Maria, consigned to some guest room, found it hard to sleep because she was frightened by the metaphysical paintings on the walls. The young couple came to Paris in 1927, and Savinio now began to paint seriously, for painting could bring in money more quickly than writing, which he had never abandoned. His first exhibition, that same year, had its catalogue prefaced by Cocteau. He did not compose new musical works at this period, for an income from music would have been even more uncertain. Raissa believed that her mother-in-law accepted *her* without too much difficulty because she came from a rich, property-owning family, therefore in the uncertain world of the mid-1920s, when hundreds of painters in Paris competed for customers, collectors and patrons, she was *persona grata.*

Although the surrealists never forgave de Chirico for painting what *he* wanted to paint and not what they believed he *ought* to paint, his work was shown during the 1920s all over the world, from New York to Berlin and Hamburg, from Brussels to London, where in the autumn of 1928 Arthur Tooth put on what was described as the 'First Exhibition in England of Paintings by Giorgio de Chirico', even though some work had been shown in Brighton in 1926. His work appeared in surrealist exhibitions, in shows of modern Italian art, in shows of French art (in Moscow), in any group where his influence, or his novelty, could be discerned. His one-man show in Brussels in 1928 was damned without mercy in *La Révolution surréaliste* (No. 11) by Raymond Queneau, not yet well known as a novelist. Like Breton in *Surrealism and Painting*, Queneau had given up hope of any return to work comparable to that of the pre-war and wartime years: 'It's useless dwelling on the great painter Giorgio de Chirico. A beard has grown on his face; an old copyist's beard; the dirty old beard of a renegade, the dirty, old colourless beard of an old man.' As for the counter-exhibitions staged by the surrealists, the painter dismissed them in Chapter 11 of his *Memoirs*, describing the perpetrators as 'hooligans' and 'petty delinquents'.

De Chirico's painting of the 1920s is interesting more for its biographical content than for any artistic reason. Why those endless horses by the seashore, often with segments of broken classical columns, sometimes with effete young men who look incapable of handling the often beautiful animals? The artist appeared obsessed with the horses, just as in the past he had painted an infinite number of arcades and piazzas; he was surely remembering what he had read in the past about classical mythology. Raissa remembered that her husband had been impressed by a fleeting image created by a Russian poet; she had forgotten his name, but she believed he wrote of a homosexual dreaming about the eyes of his beloved 'and in the background a dark blue sea, a deserted beach and horses galloping among statues and ruined temples'. Much more convincing was the explanation advanced by Savinio: his brother had been influenced by that early classic of the tourist industry *Travels in Greece* by Pausanias, who lived during the first century AD.

Another theme developed by de Chirico in the 1920s was a new range of semi-human figures carrying within their bodies buildings, ruins, archaeological remains. They are hideously heavy, faintly cubist perhaps, but intriguing all the same. Raissa always denied that her interest in archaeology influenced her husband, and he, in his most perverse moments, would deny that Greece and its antiquities meant anything to him. Whatever its origin, he was still using this theme in the 1970s.

The 1920s were a difficult and crucial decade for de Chirico. If he never stopped painting, his critics never stopped attacking him, and André Breton even continued to do so in his autobiographical novel *Nadja*, published in 1928. Breton's attitude was that of a schoolmaster who was not prepared for anyone to be independent: it was against the rules, *his* rules, formulated by him, as *chef d'école*. The 'hooligans' and 'petty delinquents' behaved like schoolboys sticking pins in insects: one magazine appeared with black edges, in mourning for de Chirico, and someone even constructed a box, an imitation coffin, inscribed 'Here lies . . .' in the time-honoured way.

De Chirico did not succeed in fighting back through his painting, and the curious so-called fighters and gladiators that they depicted seem to be caricatures, incapable of any show of strength. Even the marathon runners, remembered no doubt from the time when the schoolboy de Chirico saw the revived Olympic Games in 1896, do not run: they stand still.

Luisa Spagnoli reported a rumour that Breton, who enjoyed fighting, both ideological and physical, had once knocked de Chirico down in the street and left him unconscious on the pavement. The painter, who had grown up during a war, was never interested in fighting, but his wife maintained he never lost his repressed violence and sometimes tried to express it by continually throwing stones into a well or a pool of water. But as the decade continued he behaved even more oddly, by developing an unexpected passion for watching boxing matches and insisting that Raissa accompanied him. She saw that her husband was more affected by the critics than he admitted and had begun to wonder if his inspiration had deserted him. At the same time, she realized, too, that their happiness in marriage was affected.

The deceptively peaceable de Chirico had earlier attracted the attention of poets such as Philippe Soupault and Paul Eluard, who had both dedicated poems to him, and he was surely more pleased than he ever admitted when he again began to receive the support of writers whose interest in him was not expressed in destructive reviews, for, despite all the harsh words of the surrealists, the last few years of the 1920s produced a few voices in support of the 'renegade' painter, who had already developed into the 'monomachist' – he who fights alone – a term he had first used in 1922 in a fragment that remained unpublished until 1980 and which occurs again in the *Memoirs*. Roger Vitrac's booklet *Georges de Chirico*, No. 29 in the series *Les Peintres Français Nouveaux*, was published in 1927. First in the series had been Matisse, and comparatively few of the other names have been forgotten today. Francis Carco wrote about Utrillo, André Salmon about Derain, Paul Reverdy about Picasso. Other subjects included Marie Laurencin, Maurice Denis, Pierre Bonnard, Odilon Redon and Claude Monet. The sixty-four-page booklet on de Chirico included twenty-nine reproductions (in black and white), nineteen of them of works since 1919, so the artist could not complain that his later paintings were ignored. Vitrac's essay was warmly imaginative, closer to poetry than to analysis, and there was a significant 'P.S. Nothing authorizes me to doubt de Chirico's recent work. Nothing. On the contrary.'

Fifty years later the only 'doubt' hovers over the self-portrait line drawing of the artist on the cover of Vitrac's booklet, reproduced as a wood engraving. His large eyes look deeply unhappy and perplexed, his full lips are set in what could be described as a grin-and-bear-it expression, while his chin has become double. The 'melancholy' and 'mystery' are there, and de Chirico had clearly failed to assert himself. His attempts to respond to criticism by writing angry letters to the press – one of these was included by Breton in *Surrealism and Painting* – had also failed, and he may secretly have begun to suspect that he was no longer the great painter he so desperately wanted to be. As a result he attempted to find reassurance by convincing himself that he was just that and that it was stupid of other people not to accept the fact. These were beliefs that he maintained ever more firmly for the rest of his life.

And in 1928 he received confirmation of his greatness from two of his contemporaries. The French critic Waldemar George published *Chirico, avec des fragments littéraires de l'artiste*, and in it he made an intensely quotable reference to Picasso and de Chirico as 'the two principal events of the twentieth century'. If Picasso still remains one of them, de Chirico has a different place of his own, for he was an important precursor of surrealism, and surely that movement changed the course of the art world, for a close look at the outstanding work of the 1920s and 1930s by the surrealist painters, writers and creators easily proves that the so-called innovations of the late twentieth century are hardly new at all.

The same year saw the stirring essay by Jean Cocteau which made me take a closer look at everything that de Chirico had painted and written. Cocteau had got to know the two de Chirico brothers when they had first come to Paris in the pre-war days: Savinio first, in 1910, and Giorgio the following year. It is not clear why Cocteau decided to write that long 'essay in indirect criticism', *Le Mystère laïc* (*The Lay Mystery*), later included in his *Poésie critique*, but it was well known that the surrealists hated him, for they regarded him as a rich man's son who borrowed their ideas and made money out of them. And, since he knew that the surrealists now hated de Chirico, he may have seen an opportunity for one of his characteristic paradoxical attempts to defend the indefensible. He surely did not write the piece out of the kindness of his heart, especially when one remembers what his former admirer Maurice Sachs said of him – he had 'no heart' – but he was useful to the artists' colony in Paris, who needed a publicity agent. It could be that Cocteau had discovered someone else, de Chirico, who had 'no heart'.

Cocteau's long essay is illuminating and readable for its own sake, while near the end he seems to grasp the essence of de Chirico's work – even the painting he had not yet produced:

> The theatrical cities of Italy possess no theatres, apart from the opera, for lack of an audience. Plays are performed in the street.
>
> Chirico, the typical man of the theatre, inhibited by *bel canto*, expresses himself elsewhere: in Paris, in Greek, on canvas, just as gangsters, all of them Italian, express in America the Italy of Machiavelli, the Renaissance, blood, assassinations, coats of mail, effeminate killers, poisons, acts of daring and trickery.

He also said that de Chirico was not a literary painter: 'Eccentric, if you wish, but literary, no. A poet who paints, yes. Picasso is a painter who appears to write. De Chirico, a poet who seems to paint.'

The first edition of Cocteau's long essay included five chromolithographs by de Chirico. Cocteau had fared better than Breton, who had never received the drawings that de Chirico had promised him in the days of their friendship. Characteristically, de Chirico wrote later that he was grateful to Cocteau but that he did 'not approve of the kind of praise he accords me and the interpretation he likes to put on my pictures'.

The year 1928 may have been a busy one for critics writing about de Chirico, but the artist himself, while continuing to paint, moved into other areas of creativity. Diaghilev, constantly searching for new composers, choreographers, artists and dancers for his Ballets Russes, invited the Italian-born composer Vittorio Rieti, who lived in Paris, to write a ballet score for his company. Diaghilev took such a personal, critical interest in the work – *Le Bal* – that he repeatedly asked for changes and improvements. In the end Rieti sent him the score on 27 February 1929 and wrote, 'Here is *Le Bal*. It is dedicated to you. Do what you like with it, but don't expect me to do any more work on it.'

Diaghilev now looked for a suitable designer, and finally he chose de Chirico, who had done similar work for the Alfredo Casella–Rolf de Maré ballet *La Jarre* in 1924 and for his brother's *La Morte di Niobe* at the Teatrino degli Undici in 1925. The contract de Chirico signed with Diaghilev required him to produce sketches in oils (which were destined for the collection of stage designs being assembled by Serge Lifar), and he was also to supervise the painting of the sets at Monte Carlo, where the work was to be premièred in the summer of 1929.

The story had been devised by Boris Kochno, Diaghilev's artistic adviser, from a tale by the neglected Russian writer Vladimir Sologub, who had died in 1927; Kochno described it as 'a poetic episode set in the Romantic period, having a mysterious and unearthly character which few people appreciated at the time'. Obviously there was an affinity with some of de Chirico's work. The story was set in Russia in the early 1800s, and if the chosen designer had never seen the country he had a Russian wife and many Russian friends. But de Chirico had his own ideas about what was 'mysterious and unearthly', with the result that the decor and costumes were close to his current work but irrelevant to what is usually understood as 'the Romantic period'. Kochno said that 'without recreating a definite period style de Chirico devised a mise-en-scène that suggested a masked ball and accentuated the phantom-like aspect of the ballet's character'.

The curtain went up to show the façade of a house with 'two gigantic naked male figures – one playing cymbals, the other dancing', as Richard Buckle wrote. A brilliant cast, including Anton Dolin, Alexandra Danilova, Lifar, and Georges Balanchine, the choreographer, performed this story of love and magic during a masked ball which took place in the second tableau. Danilova later recalled 'angular' poses and 'very syncopated steps'. The artist's main contribution to the ballroom scene included a mysterious figure who seemed to embody a memory of his father, while the young man beside him seemed reminiscent of himself, recalling the return of the Prodigal Son which he had often painted. The costumes carried appliqué motifs adapted from classical architecture – scrolls, triumphal arches, Ionic capitals – while Lifar appeared astride a cardboard white horse. The walls of the ballroom were 'marbled and so was the material of the costumes, which gave their wearers the air of animated statues'. The whole of de Chirico was there, and this curious amalgam, with its element of surprise, could even be described as surrealist. It was a great success, in Monte Carlo, Paris, Berlin and London. Raissa, who accompanied her husband to the Paris première, remembered that during the applause, standing in their box, he called out, 'You've forgotten the principal person – me!'

In London, the *Morning Post* review said of the Covent Garden performance that 'It pleased everybody of every section of opinion. It was certainly the most successful novelty of the last few years.' Lydia Lopokova, writing in the *Nation and Athenaeum*, went further: 'The joy and beauty of this ballet is [*sic*] to be found in de Chirico's décor . . . this is the smartest ballet we have seen for many seasons.' It was also the end of an era. The last performance at the Royal Opera House took place on 29 July 1929. On 19 August Diaghilev died in Venice.

The Ballets Russes had experienced immense artistic success and constant shortage of money. But by the autumn of 1929 virtually everyone was short of money, owing to the Wall Street crash. In Paris nobody bought paintings any more, and de Chirico and his wife were forced to leave their apartment in the rue Meissonier in the seventeenth arrondissement and move to a smaller one in the rue Lacretelle in a less elegant area, off the rue de Vaugirard in the fifteenth. Presumably even the ex-colonel Vladimir was sacked.

It was the painter's bad luck that this year saw the publication of his major literary work, the surrealist novel *Hebdomeros*. Can there be such a thing as a 'surrealist novel'? Is it a contradiction in terms? No matter. Breton's *Nadja* of the previous year is part fiction, part imaginative memoir and part prose-poem, moving and unforgettable, even if the *chef d'école* could not refrain from returning in it to his regrets about de Chirico's abandonment of his earlier style. When review copies of *Hebdomeros* were sent out they contained an unusually poetic explanatory blurb attributed to the author: 'Hebdomeros is the peaceable phantom, the luminous spectre of Giorgio de Chirico, Dante and Virgil combined in one person . . .'

Hebdomeros is a poetic book, full of direct memories of the author's childhood and much more besides – his reading and his unresolved philosophical quest. It is also in many ways a pessimistic book, full of irony and even cynicism but ending with the tacit admission that the mystery of existence, the enigma – the word does not appear in the book – cannot be solved. Hebdomeros has to learn that existence will continue for ever but without him. Perhaps the author was contemplating the 'metaphysical' longevity of his own work, if not his own life. The novel ends with a much-quoted passage with an autobiographical content and an unexpected touch of humour:

> All at once, Hebdomeros saw that this woman had his father's eyes; and he *understood*. She spoke of immortality, in the great starless night.
>
> 'Oh, Hebdomeros,' she said, 'I am Immortality. Names have their gender, or rather their sex, as you once said with much finesse, and verbs, alas, are declined. Have you ever thought of my death? Have you ever thought about the death of my death? Have you ever *thought about my life?*'

And there follow a few more lines of peaceable meditation.

Even the surrealists admired this novel; it looked as though de Chirico could now express himself in metaphysical style by using words rather than paint. Analysis of the book could easily fill another volume, and I myself have spent much rewarding time correlating its imagery with that of the paintings. De Chirico wrote many poems, mainly short, but paradoxically his poetry is found more convincingly in his prose. Cocteau admired the book – predictably. Predictably, too, it did not sell.

Two years later, in early 1931, the painter-poet and his wife were invited to dinner, in company with other painters, by the young, still unknown Léonor Fini, whom de Chirico had persuaded to come to Paris from Rome. Gregorio Sciltian and his wife were among the guests. As they were about to take their places at table Lily Sciltian noticed that they were a group of thirteen.

7
The 'Most Profoundly Intelligent Person'

SEVERAL of the guests were no doubt superstitious, and de Chirico himself was always said to be so. As a result, Lily Sciltian went to find her friend and neighbour Isabella Pakszwer, who lived in the apartment below, and persuaded her to join the party. As the alfresco meal proceeded, the fourteen people found they had drunk all the wine in the Fini establishment. It was Isabella, the latecomer, who volunteered to go out and buy some more. De Chirico volunteered to accompany her. They did not come back.

Raissa soon realized that her marriage was over. She was particularly hurt because, following the world financial crisis she had helped to finance her husband's work and exhibitions, while she could hardly have enjoyed living in the rue Lacretelle, as they now did. In the spring of 1931 de Chirico was due to go to an exhibition in Brussels, where his work was on show, but he could not afford the railway fare. Raissa was still a helpful wife: she apparently pawned some of her jewellery on his behalf, and he went to Belgium. She could not say at this stage that her husband behaved well. She had always known him to be timid, and now he could not face her. He went into hiding, staying with friends, apparently, or in the studio which he still used in the rue Henri-Bocquillon. This was not the first time he had broken away from conventional married behaviour, for Raissa had noticed his interest in a Romanian girl who had attended the boxing matches he had liked to watch. Raissa even maintained that this girl appeared in the novel *Hebdomeros* and that de Chirico had written poems to her. Raissa also believed that her husband had always been something of a romantic and, if he had stopped visiting brothels when he fell in love with her, she thought he had once been fascinated by a prostitute who frequented the Café de la Paix.

After his meeting with Isabella, de Chirico not only went to Brussels with the help of his wife's money, he also stayed away a long time. Raissa began to worry, and so did his mother and brother. Raissa had always known that her husband needed someone – preferably a woman – to tell him what to do, as his mother had always done, and she felt now that she herself had not conducted her side of the marriage partnership as she should have done. She had not told Giorgio what to do – or so she thought. Did she remember what her first husband had told her: 'Don't trust an Italian'? But she had: she had believed her Italian lover; she had believed what he had said in that letter she kept all her life – he had said that everything would be for her. Eventually a new letter reached her from Milan, where in May 1931 de Chirico had a show, saying that he would not be coming back to live with her; he would be living alone. Apparently he then repeated what he had said in 1925: all his life he would work for her. This was hardly true, although years later, when she was ill, she would receive some financial help from him, although never enough.

Her studies in archaeology at the Sorbonne helped her now; she soon returned to Italy and there met a leading archaeologist, Guido Calza, whom she married. They worked together on archaeological excavations at Ostia Antica.

Isabella Pakszwer had been born in Poland into a well-off Jewish family. Her father, who owned a textile business, arranged for her to be educated in Moscow, where she lived with an aunt. Isabella was a beautiful young woman with a lovely skin and magnificent fair hair. She was also highly ambitious, telling her childhood friend Lily that she wanted to marry an ambassador and own lots of jewellery and furs. When Lily married Gregorio Sciltian in Berlin, Isabella thought she had made a poor match, having chosen a mere painter for her husband. Lily maintained that her friend knew nothing whatever about art, and Isabella seems to have been a strange creature, 'shy and solitary, always dissatisfied with everything and happy only in the company of older men and homosexuals'. Disliking also young people and children, Isabella seems to have been a kind of unnatural, artificial woman. 'De Chirico,' wrote Luisa Spagnoli, no doubt quoting either Lily or Raissa, 'was her first man; she had not had other love affairs earlier, and apparently their sexual relationship did not work well.' The only real women that de Chirico had painted had been in portraits, for which he was influenced by Renoir; in his earlier work he had preferred statues and sexless beings, some of which eventually acquired vaguely feminine attributes. After all those artificial women in his pictures – the marble goddesses, the mannequins and the muses – he had now found a living 'artificial' woman for himself.

There is no mention of Raissa in his *Memoirs*. Apparently, Isabella had said that if he wrote about his first wife she would kill herself. So, as Raissa had always said he would, he did as he was told, by a woman. There are more references in his *Memoirs* to Isabella than to any one else, even his parents and his brother. She was 'the most profoundly intelligent person', he maintained.

De Chirico's domestic problems do not seem to have lasted very long, and in any case he never stopped painting. Galleries all over the world continued to include his work in exhibitions of all kinds; on average, during 1931 and 1932 he figured in about fifteen exhibitions a month, varying from one-man shows in Milan, Florence, London, Düsseldorf and Prague to collective shows in Chicago, New York, Geneva, Amsterdam, Antwerp and Vienna. In 1934 the Paris surrealist review *Minotaure* included some of his old work in an exhibition in Brussels at the Palais des Beaux-Arts, a few months after issue No. 5 of that fascinating magazine had included a colour frontispiece of de Chirico's *The Duo* of 1915. The same issue included his intriguing prose piece 'On Silence' and a woodcut of his 1914 drawing of Apollinaire. (*Minotaure* Nos. 8 (1936), 10 (1937) and 12/13 (May 1939) also included reproductions of his work.) The prose piece, in a style close to that which he had used in *Hebdomeros*, ranged from God's creation of the world, in silence, to a glimpse of 'gentlemen poets' writing platonic sonnets, ending with an evocation of a boxing match and a sudden gust of wind that blew sheets of paper out of the window. The painter-writer spent years fulminating against the surrealists in articles and in his *Memoirs* – denouncing them as 'impotent intellectuals', 'hysterical, 'hydrophobic' and suffering from the 'modernist virus' – but, at this stage at least, he apparently did not try to stop them reproducing work by him which they regarded as surrealist even if he did not.

De Chirico was far from idle in other fields. He often said later in life that he did not really care for working in the theatre, but he constantly did so. After his contribution to the ballet *Le Bal*, Serge Lifar had realized his potential as a designer and had asked de Chirico to collaborate with him in *Bacchus et Ariane*, which he had devised for the Paris Opéra in 1931. This was an avant-garde work, with a libretto by Abel Hermant and a score by Albert Roussel. Lifar himself, in his 1965 book *La Danse*, described it as 'very daring through its eroticism, its tension and its *plastique*'. The audience hated de Chirico's drop curtain and were not impressed by the gloves worn by Ariadne (danced by Olga Spessivtseva) nor the high boots worn by Lifar as Bacchus. (André Levinson, the erudite ballet critic, meanwhile, was also not impressed by the choreography nor by the general adaptation of the classical legend.)

De Chirico had even less success with his designs for Vincenzo Bellini's famous 1834 opera *I Puritani*, produced a century later at the 1933 Maggio Musicale in Florence. Had he forgotten that seventeenth-century English Puritans wore simple, not outlandish, clothes? Was he perhaps more concerned with his memories of metaphysical painting than with the history underlying the plot of the opera? De Chirico complained that the director of the newspaper *La Nazione* organized an attack on his designs because he had not wanted to hold an exhibition on the paper's premises. In Chapter 12 of his *Memoirs*, he wrote:

> I wanted to exhibit at the Palazzo Ferroni, since this gallery belonged to one of my good friends, the antique dealer Luigi Bellini, who was also my host. In order to have his revenge for the fact that I had not exhibited in the newspaper office room the director gave orders that

> my sets and costumes should be booed during the show and later ridiculed and attacked in the newspaper by the official critics; naturally, large troops of volunteers, composed of painters and intellectuals, spontaneously offered the director some help in his noble vendetta.

De Chirico had at least one eminent supporter, the German theatrical producer Max Reinhardt, who apparently liked his work so much that he wanted him to return to London and work with him there on his forthcoming Shakespearian productions. But de Chirico declined the offer, maintaining that 'all this kind of thing did not suit me'. *I Puritani* was the first time he had designed for opera, but it was to be far from the last.

What clearly suited him, after years of seemingly timid behaviour, was the chance to have a good row. In that he resembled André Breton. But there the resemblance ended, for de Chirico was now showing what seemed to be incipient paranoia, perpetually complaining that he was badly treated. Breton, by contrast, made sure that such a thing would never happen to him: he would take positive action not at once but in advance.

In 1933 de Chirico, along with four other painters, was invited by the organizers of the fifth Milan Triennale to illustrate the theme 'Italy in its most noble and varied manifestations', and the artists were also to demonstrate the modernized reuse of old techniques. De Chirico complained that his large mural, executed in tempera, was not photographed by the press, although the work of the other artists – Mario Sironi, Gino Severini, Massimo Campigli and Achille Funi – was. He remarked that when the exhibition closed 'all the paintings . . . were destroyed, probably because they did not dare, owing to possible scandals, to destroy only mine'.

The painter described this incident in his *Memoirs*, where he also mentioned the Rome Quadriennale of 1935 (although he mistakenly gave the date as 1934). Just before the Quadriennale he had spent some time – 'assisted by Isabella's brilliant intuition' – researching earlier techniques through studying 'old treatises and writings on painting' in the Bibliothèque Nationale in Paris, and he then sent some new work, embodying his discoveries, to the Rome exhibition. He later complained bitterly of 'hysterical anger' in press campaigns against him. He mentioned that Mussolini – Il Duce – had shown interest in his work but had not been allowed to linger in front of it. In fact he wrote personally to the Duce from Paris on 18 February 1935. He told him that 'at his [Mussolini's] wish' everything in Italy, 'in both the material and spiritual spheres', had been encouraged and supported, but he, de Chirico, was 'boycotted and persecuted by the intrigues of envious critics'. He wanted to know if efforts were being made to prevent him from winning the first prize or to stop the state acquiring any of his works. De Chirico later asserted that he was not hoping that Mussolini would arrange for him to receive the first prize at the Quadriennale (it was in fact awarded to Severini), but at least one of de Chirico's oil paintings, *Combattimento di Gladiatori* (*Gladiators Fighting*), was bought for the Galleria Communale. The gladiators in this work look as if they are posing for a photograph of men who have been pretending to fight or are thinking of doing so. The kindest attitude to take to this painting, and others in the same style, is to assume that the intention was ironic in some way difficult for others to understand. De Chirico wrote in the catalogue for the Quadriennale that others of the forty-five works he showed in the room allocated to him had been influenced to some extent by his theatrical work. It is hard to discern a theatrical quality in *The Mysterious Baths*, *The Swimmer* or *The Mysterious Swan*, but these were the themes he mentioned.

He had remained in Paris during the period of the Quadriennale, but he was soon 'disgusted by the low level, material and moral, to which painting in Paris had sunk'. He decided, spurred on by 'a friend' and no doubt by Isabella (now his wife), that he should go to the USA, for his work had been popular there. He was to be met by Isabella's uncle and aunt, who lived there, and she would join him later.

He arrived in the USA in August 1935, and at first, with his usual perversity, he 'felt a great nostalgia for Europe'. He missed the architecture which had made such a contribution to his paintings, for in the

USA 'Those smooth, monotonous buildings, from which protruded no balcony, no capital or column, no cornice, no ornament, no pole or nail, alarmed me greatly.' However, the trip was worthwhile for the visiting artist, for 'dollars poured in'.

The few pages he wrote in his *Memoirs* (Chapter 13) about his time in the USA give some idea of his activities, his opinions of Julien Levy, who organized an important show for him in the autumn of 1936, and his view of Dr Alfred Barnes, who owned twenty-five of his paintings and seemed to have some affinities with the painter, for the method he used 'to attract the attention of his contemporaries towards his museum consists in being as contrary and misanthropic as humanly possible'. He mentioned the work he did for *Vogue* and *Harpers*, including a cover for the former, but he did not like the 'atmosphere' of the magazines. He did not mention a window display for the outfitters Scheiner, which included 'Petronius and modern Adonis in evening dress' with a few segments of classical columns and a de Chirico-style skyscraper in the background. Nor did he mention the twelve-foot-high mural he designed for the Helena Rubinstein beauty institute, showing mythological people, gods and horses on a beach. The architectural review *Domus* described his achievements in the USA; the Pierre Matisse Gallery gave him his first major New York show in the autumn of 1935; and his work – admittedly the early, so-called surrealist paintings – appeared in many exhibitions all over North America.

In the meantime, during his absence from Europe, the New Burlington Gallery in London put on the important International Surrealist Exhibition in 1936. André Breton was photographed standing beside the picture by de Chirico that he had bought when still young, *The Child's Brain*, but Breton had not had the chance to supervise the show and he complained that one work by de Chirico (probably one of the 'Tower' paintings) included the Italian flag – green, white and red – and that, to the left-wing Breton, represented the symbol of Fascism.

In the month when this show closed, July 1936, the painter received sad news from his brother: their mother was ill; then, their mother was dead. 'One night,' wrote the precursor of surrealism, 'I had a dream; I dreamt I was in Greece . . . I saw those trees and bushes which I had seen during my childhood . . .' He saw everything again – the olives, the pine trees, the 'little church painted pink'.

> Suddenly my mother appeared among the olives and walked towards the little church. I wanted to go and meet her, but I could not move . . . I saw my mother, who seemed very old, small, bent, weak and unsteady on her feet, just as I remembered her from the last time I had seen her in Paris. I saw my mother pass like a shadow near the apse of the little church, come up to the side door and then disappear.

Ten days later he received the news from his brother: his mother had died precisely at the time when he had had this dream.

The two brothers reacted to their mother's death in different ways. Savinio wrote the moving fantasy 'My Mother Doesn't Understand Me' in *Casa 'La Vita'*, to which his elder brother referred later in his *Memoirs*. Giorgio had painted her many times, and he had painted the relationship between them, but he did not return to Italy for her funeral. When he go back, in 1938, he had intended to have a splendid tomb built in her memory, but according to Luisa Spagnoli the idea faded from his mind and the tomb was never built. However, with the help of Savinio's story, more memorable than his fantasy-portraits, plus Cocteau's one-sentence reference to her in *The Lay Mystery* – 'their mother, wearing full evening dress, seated on a ballroom chair, with a bouquet of roses in her hand' – the Baronessa has attained immortality. Cocteau also wrote that she supervised her sons 'from an Acropolis'; thus he expressed the reality, and the unreality, of the family situation.

By the end of 1937 de Chirico decided that he was tired of the USA. In New York he could not feel the *Stimmung* of autumn, 'that strange, distant and profound poetry that Nietzsche discovered in the clear autumn afternoons, especially when they lie over certain Italian cities such as Turin'. As for his work, the American critics had written articles 'not very intelligent but fairly favourable', although, like his critics everywhere, they 'had understood nothing of the *quality* of my pictures and spoke only about the subject matter'. So early in January 1938 – not 1937, as recorded in the *Memoirs* – he and Isabella moved to Rome, via Naples. Once back in Italy he wrote interestingly about the USA in *L'Illustrazione Italiana* on 13 February. On the west side of the Gulf Stream, he thought, is another world:

> it is America . . . When New York appears you think of the remains of vanished cities built by people who had reached a high level of mechanical perfection; you think of Pompeii, of Babylon and of certain reconstructions of Imperial Rome made by German archaeologists. If you are asked what you think of all this it's difficult to give an answer; it is another world; it is the Metaphysics of America. A strange power and a strange impassibility; mechanical complexity . . . Shop windows predominate in New York; there seems to be an exhibition everywhere; in the shop windows of New York the whole history of humanity is displayed every day. I have seen shop windows in 57th Street with lay figures representing elegant women seated among a kind of collective reconstruction of my paintings with horses from the ancient world, fragments of columns, temples, porticoes and vistas. [This was presumably not the Scheiner display, but it is not clear what it does refer to.] The Americans have a shop window culture, a culture of things displayed; moreover the houses with their windows bare of curtains and shades look like shop windows; passing by late at night you can see men playing cards, women reading, talking or listening to the radio like automata and ghosts . . .

In the same issue of the magazine he also wrote enthusiastically about Rome, for in the Italian 'reawakening' under Mussolini he was now aware of superior discipline, respect for man, honour, dignity, work. In a secure atmosphere, in a new and free 'Athens', works of art would be more beautiful. This might have been construed by some as an appreciation of all that Mussolini had achieved so far. In November 1937 Savinio had written to the newspaper *Il Meridiano di Roma* in order to quash rumours that the de Chirico family were Jewish. He pointed out their long Catholic history, but not everyone was convinced, for when Giorgio offered to teach in a state academy, even free of charge, he was treated with indifference. A further sign of his unpopularity occurred when stones were thrown at a bookshop where his novel *Hebdomeros* was on sale. Since Giorgio, unlike his brother, remained aloof from anti-Fascist circles, these incidents showed how, in his words, 'black clouds were growing denser over the sky of Europe'. There was an added problem: that 'most profoundly intelligent person' Isabella was Jewish, and both she and her husband became aware of the threats they might encounter.

However, the immediate pre-war period was a time 'when things went well' for de Chirico. Perhaps he had gained confidence – if he ever needed it – after a special trip to Milan in 1938 in order to consult a medium named Morosini, who was apparently very successful. 'My son,' said the medium immediately after going into a trance, 'you are one of the most envied men in the world!' Apparently de Chirico often remembered those words. He held successful shows in both Paris and London, although the surrealists in the French capital made no secret of considering him as dead. When compiling his *Memoirs*, de Chirico became experienced in writing detailed accounts of his successes and merely blaming external factors for any failure.

In July 1938 his work could be seen in two London galleries. Some early paintings were included in a mainly surrealist show at the London Gallery, entitled 'The Impact of Machines', but he did not mention this in his *Memoirs*. However, in Chapter 14 he wrote that 'the Lefevre Gallery in London, a more serious and less futile place than most of the galleries showing modern paintings, gave a one-man show of my recent paintings'. He went to London, since he was also due to attend the première on 5 July of a new ballet at Covent Garden, for which he had designed the sets and costumes. This was *Protée*, with choreography by David Lichine and music by Debussy. He recorded with pleasure the success of the ballet, after which he had 'had to come on stage to acknowledge the applause, holding the prima ballerina's damp fingers in my right hand and the equally damp fingers of the premier danseur in my left'. He was also pleased to be invited to supper afterwards at the Savoy, 'the smartest hotel in London'.

As in New York, he reacted to the special atmosphere he found in London:

> London in summer is extraordinarily metaphysical; Jules Verne has expressed magnificently, but perhaps unconsciously, the metaphysical quality of London, when he described Phileas Fogg's return to the capital after his adventurous trip round the world in eighty days . . . During my stay in London I lived through hours of profound metaphysical sensation, especially on Sunday afternoons when I went for walks alone, alongside the Thames . . .

Old memories returned to him: 'As I walked along I thought of my father, my mother, my distant childhood, of so many things that still follow me through life with the distant beating of the wings of memory.'

On his return to Italy he and Isabella were living in Milan. Once back, he had a more mundane success: in passing his driving test, having failed in an earlier attempt in Paris. Isabella passed, too. But the atmosphere in Milan was not metaphysical but anti-Semitic, so they went back to Paris but soon fled again to Cannes, Vichy and Nice. These journeys took up the last months of 1939 and the earlier part of 1940, when they returned to Milan.

In the meantime André Breton had published his entertaining *Anthology of Black Humour* during the period of *la drôle de guerre*, the 'phoney war'; but no sooner was the Vichy government installed in 1940 than its officials decided the book was offensive and banned it. The surrealists were in any case considered as subversive, and Breton's introductory pieces to his selected authors emphasized the fact. Only one Italian writer was included – Savinio, represented by an amusing and ironic extract from *Introduction to a Life of Mercury*, originally written in French and first published in Paris at the end of 1929. Breton's introduction to this anthology is still relevant. He stated that 'the entire modern myth, still in formation, was based on the work of Alberto Savinio and his brother Giorgio de Chirico', whose natures were 'practically indistinguishable'. He quoted Savinio's remarks about 'the metaphysical idea' moving from 'the state of abstraction to that of the senses' and referred to *The Songs of Half-Death* and their link with Giorgio's painting. He also made a straightforward reference to motifs in the painter's work: 'the interplay of towers, and arcades . . . expressing the relationship between the male and female sexes'. Lastly, he mentioned Hebdomeros, whose attitude to 'moral and immoral foods' was reminiscent of Freud's theories concerning oral consumption.

Giorgio, for obvious reasons, was not included in the anthology, but Savinio, in the preface to his *Tutta la Vita* (1945), referred to what Breton had said and commented on it. Savinio did not see surrealism as something that sought to represent what was formless and to express the unconscious: he himself in his writing and painting wished to endow the formless with form and the unconscious with the conscious. His statement may or may not have made his position, and that of his brother, more clear. Breton, meanwhile, along with Max Ernst and many other surrealists, had left France in 1941 for the USA, where he continued to direct surrealist activities.

Chapters 15 and 16 of de Chirico's *Memoirs* give a fair impression of how two middle-aged people lived through the early, confused, years of the war and the changed scene when in 1943 Mussolini was dismissed by the King. Marshal Badoglio then arranged a peace with France and Britain but declared war on Germany. This new situation lasted until the final peace of 1945, and the Italian Republic was declared in May 1946.

During the six years of the war – most of them spent in Milan – de Chirico and Isabella were far from idle. He experimented with small-scale terracotta sculptures, assisted by a professional. He also presented a show of his brother's work in Milan in 1940 and produced during the following year twenty lithographs for a new edition of the Apocalypse (from the the Book of Revelation), with commentary by his friend Massimo Bontempelli. In 1942 de Chirico designed scenery and costumes for a ballet at La Scala, *Anfione*, based on Paul Valéry's poem 'Amphion', but the painter's work was not well received.

Exhibitions including his work, or one-man shows, continued to take place, one of the most interesting being the New York show of works from the Peggy Guggenheim collection in 1943.

The following year saw crucial events in the war: Monte Cassino, Anzio, the Normandy landings, the execution of Count Ciano, after trial for his defection from the Fascist regime, on the orders of his father-in-law, Mussolini. It was hardly surprising that exhibitions of any kind were few, and de Chirico was lucky to have four – two in Milan and two in Rome. In July 1944 his prose fragment entitled 'Sensitiveness' was published in the London literary review *Horizon*. There was no editorial comment, no indication of its origin, but its message was predictable – 'sensitiveness, I maintain, when applied to a work of art *does not exist*. And when someone, speaking of a picture, tells me that it *shows sensitiveness*, I can only reply that I am ready to believe as much, but only on condition that it can be proven.' There are also two short paragraphs about sincerity as well as sensitiveness: 'critics and intellectuals' and also 'modernist painters', says de Chirico, have used these jargon words 'with the express purpose of rendering the stupidity and confusion already reigning in the minds of men even more acute'.

Although listed as his own work in the bibliography of de Chirico's writings, this piece may have been due to the new activity of Isabella, who, as Isabella Far, had taken to writing articles about various aspects of art which her husband then signed, presumably in a further bid to catch the eye of the critics and fight back, as was to be expected. After all, had he not painted himself dressed as a bullfighter two years earlier? A little later Isabella's articles were collected and published in book form, under her own name. Her husband found it strange that her work was greeted with 'hysterical silence', even though it merely expressed his own well-known ideas, of which there seemed to be two: first, modernist painters and critics were all useless intellectuals, all failures, and they knew nothing – even Mussolini was a failed writer, that is a would-be intellectual, a form of life he despised; second, he himself was *Pictor Optimus*, the best painter, whom nobody understood.

It was Isabella, apparently, who decreed that the phrase *natura morta*, or *nature morte* for the French, should be abolished and the words *vita silente*, 'silent life', be used instead. Her preferred phrase is at least closer to the English term. In 1945 de Chirico painted *Vita Silente di uccelli con canestro* (*Silent Life of Birds with Hamper*), in which the birds are not only silent, they are dead.

De Chirico valued his wife: it had taken him a long time to come to terms with the existence of women, but he was surely as happy now as he would ever be. He painted Isabella many times, in the nude, by the sea, or wearing a leopardskin coat and hat as *The Skater* in 1941. In *The Friends* or *The Sisters-in-Law* of the same year she looks out of the picture and meets our eyes. She is affectionately rejuvenated and pretty, with a slightly triangular face, while her sister-in-law, Maria Savinio, is seen in profile, looking modestly downward.

In 1945 de Chirico ended the first edition of his *Memoirs* by saying that when he was not painting he consoled himself 'by reading the writings of Isabella Far'. On the same page he referred to her 'philosophical acumen, descriptive strength, logic, clarity, efficacy, in fact *talent*'. He added that all this 'can only find an equivalent in the times of Arthur Schopenhauer'. This 'most profoundly intelligent person', Isabella, had also, it appears, 'almost finished a very fine novel which is an intellectual, political and moral critique of our time'. It does not seem to have been completed or published.

He had been lucky on that evening in Paris some fifteen years earlier. He had found, more or less by accident, the woman whose existence he had foreseen in his painting, especially during the Ferrara years. He had traversed the period when the Muses were disquieting, and now he was safe from them. The only unlucky person had been the blue-eyed, plump Raissa. She had realized that de Chirico needed a mother replacement, which she herself had failed to provide, and after her divorce she had hoped that Isabella would at least ensure that de Chirico the painter would not disintegrate. But how far was this second partner responsible for the current state of his work?

8
Et Quid Amabo Nisi Quod Rerum Metaphysica Est?

DE Chirico and Isabella had returned to Rome in 1944, living first in the via Gregoriana and later in the via Mario dei'Fiori. His paintings were shown in several exhibitions that year and the next, including participation in a surrealist show in Brussels. The first part of his autobiography was published in 1945, his novel *Hebdomeros* was translated into Italian, he published the first few pages of what was intended to be a new novel, and rumours began to circulate about fake de Chirico paintings.

It has been estimated that during a career lasting from 1910 until his death in 1978 some 4,000–5,000 easel paintings were ascribed to de Chirico, not counting drawings, book illustrations, sculpture and designs for the theatre. Yet many of these works may have been copies he made himself or even forgeries of one kind or another. The critic Maurizio Fagiolo dell'Arco sees the painting as divided into twelve periods. The important stages, the only ones recognized by many other critics and art historians, were of course the early and later metaphysical periods, lasting from 1910 to 1918. The years from 1937 to 1948, which includes the time of his return to Rome, constitute the 'baroque-romantic' period, to be followed by the last, the 'neo-metaphysical' painting of 1948–78.

'Baroque' was indeed a good description of the work he carried out during the war and for a few years after, including another series of intriguing, perhaps even alarming, self-portraits. There is a choice of themes: the artist wearing a turban and oriental dress; the artist in seventeenth-century costume; the artist as bullfighter; the artist in the nude. Was he still trying to find himself? It seems more likely that he was celebrating the fact that he *had* found himself and remained de Chirico, *Pictor Optimus*, in whatever guise, or disguise, he appeared: he could do whatever he liked. Dr Palma Bucarelli, however, writing in *L'Indipendente* in May 1945, decided that de Chirico had 'fallen into the most chaotic disorder'. His interest in materials for their own sake was, she thought, 'artistically absurd' and the result was pastiche – forgery in fact. She thought that de Chirico simply did not know how to paint. His technique was 'uncertain and approximate' – like that of a 'popular' painter, although lacking any ingenuous quality. She referred in particular to the nude *Self-Portrait* of 1945 (possibly begun in 1942), saying that, although it was more or less possible to count the hairs on the painter's shaggy chest, the draughtsmanship was clumsy and inadequate. Was this 'great joker', as she called him, really playing a joke? If he was, the joke had lasted 'too long'.

The de Chirico ménage made their final move in 1947, to a house in the piazza di Spagna, number 31. The painter was now becoming something of a tourist attraction in himself, and he had already begun to attract even more attention in the press through his anger over the discovery of fakes. In July 1946 the Galerie Allard in Paris organized an exhibition of works from before the First World War to the 1920s, but the artist himself announced that none of them was genuine. Perhaps this was his revenge on the people who persisted in praising his early work and denouncing anything done later. From now on the question of fake de Chiricos never vanished from the press or, later, from the law courts.

It was arranged that if the authenticity of any work was in doubt de Chirico would personally sign any genuine painting that was shown to him. According to Luisa Spagnoli, there would often be a near-farcical scene at the painter's residence. Whenever anyone arrived with a doubtful painting, the maestro would glance at it and transmit a coded signal to his wife, whereupon she would telephone the appropriate section of the fraud squad. Police officers would then come to the house and confiscate the painting – for it was nearly always a fake. Between the arrival of the painting and its departure de Chirico would apparently attempt to entertain the 'owner', supposedly even humming a little song:

> I like Gide, I like Claudel,
> But I prefer crème caramel.

Sometimes he would make a mistake and fail to recognize a genuine de Chirico, and on at least one occasion he had to compensate a gallery owner falsely accused of fraud.

At this period the paintings could be conveniently divided into four groups: the genuine, the fake, the quasi-genuine and the quasi-fake. Some genuine works had not been signed but were passed by the maestro. It was hard to prove that the 'fakes' were truly fakes, produced by fraudulent painters, for the owners could often quote galleries or third parties or say they had inherited the work after the death of a relative. As for the 'quasi-genuine' works, this group included the many paintings carried out by the maestro himself and duly signed but predated. These could include a *Piazza d'Italia* painted in 1956 but dated 1913 or *Furniture in the Open Air* from 1945 predated to 1929. As for the 'quasi-fakes', these were pictures planned or finished by the artist but not wholly his work. Raissa had observed this system at first hand, but painters in Italy and elsewhere had used this kind of assistance for centuries. No incident involving a possible de Chirico fake was ever neglected by the press, and some serious critics began to suggest that maybe the artist himself had kept on copying his own earlier pictures or deliberating faking new ones simply in order to make sure he was never out of the news. Readers with particular interest in the question of forged de Chirico paintings will be entertained by his own account of some of the problems involved, set out in Chapter 17 of his *Memoirs*.

Palma Bucarelli had referred to de Chirico as a possible joker, and when it suited him he would pretend that he was or, rather, had been. His painting of the years following the Second World War – 'silent lifes', landscapes, even some of the horses and especially some of the mythological scenes – are so unattractive that one could even prefer a forged 'metaphysical' work, provided the forgery was efficient.

So what had happened to the 'enigma', the search for things metaphysical? The 'enigma' seemed to be the man himself. Nearly twenty years with Isabella had brought him the kind of happiness he had never known before, for, although she organized him as his mother had done, she was not his mother, even if her word was law. Did she really care about him? Luisa Spagnoli reported her threatening to throw away copies of *Hebdomeros*, for they took up too much space in the cupboard. It was rumoured that earlier she had actually dared to sell some of her mother-in-law's valuable carpets to help finance her husband's trip to the USA. She was a practical woman, obviously, and could be contrary. Did she ever hear her husband talking to journalists and café acquaintances about sex, as Luisa Spagnoli did? She was reputed to be not very interested in it; he was reported as saying that he did not know what sexual problems were, and he thought psychology and psychoanalysis did little more than encourage gossip. His arch-enemies, Breton and the surrealists, had been deeply involved with Freudian theory; therefore for him it must inevitably be a waste of time.

No doubt other painters have worked their way through many changes of style – Picasso comes to mind at once, although he always remained Picasso, however and whatever he painted – but it is nevertheless strange to think of Giorgio de Chirico moving so far from the metaphysical and the proto-surrealist that he was delighted, in 1948, to be made a member of the Royal Society of British Artists in London. The following year the society exhibited a hundred or so of his paintings in a big one-man show, which he attended. That summer, back in Italy, he wrote at length in *Il Merlo Giallo* saying how pleased he had been: 'This exhibition has given me great satisfaction through the great interest it has aroused, and such interest has confirmed to me in full the need felt by the public today for that artistic renaissance that I have fought for over so many years.' He had given lectures in which he spoke 'of the decadence of contemporary art, illustrating the causes of it'. He had sold many paintings, he said, and 'the purchase that moved me most was that made by the best known and most quoted English critic, Eric Newton', who had praised his work highly in the *Sunday Times*. The painter added that he had kept in an album 'this record of my first crusade conducted outside Italy against falsity, impotence and deception in Art'.

The much-criticized nude *Self-Portrait* was included in the show, but this was a different version: a *perizoma*, a loincloth, had been added. Did someone advise him that the British public would otherwise be shocked? Or did he think that this concession to modesty would improve the painting? It didn't. The work was shown again in Venice later that year and displeased his 'modernist' critics so much that they tried to obstruct one of his lectures.

De Chirico was over sixty now, but nothing reduced his output, which included scene designs for Monteverdi's *Orfeo* (1949) and for a stage version of Ildebrando Pizzetti's radio opera *Ifigenia* (1951) for the Florentine Maggio Musicale, plus Richard Strauss's ballet *Legend of Joseph* at La Scala, Milan (1951). For this latter he again, as in *Le Bal*, introduced large-scale classical male nude figures and added warriors on horseback complete with plumed helmets. His theatre work continued through the 1950s, including set and costume designs for a 1956 Piccola Scala production of Stravinsky's *Apollon Musagète* with choreography by Lifar. On 2 February 1956 a Sunday newspaper, *La Domenica del Corriere*, published a whole page of illustrations showing side by side authentic and non-authentic paintings, reflecting the amount of public interest in this controversial issue. No doubt the artist was delighted with the publicity.

In 1952 there had come a sad event: the sudden death of Alberto Savinio. He had been working at the Florentine Maggio Musicale, for which he had designed the scenery and costumes for Rossini's opera *Armida*. Maria Callas was singing, and the show was a great success. The gifted Savinio died of a heart attack during the night of 5–6 May. He had recently written to the director of the Bergamo Festival, who had commissioned him to write an opera, saying how young he was feeling: he was sixty. His elder brother was heartbroken and must have felt remorse, for the two men had drifted apart – owing, it was said, to disagreements between their wives. De Chirico wrote eight pages of sorrowful epitaph for his brother in the second edition of his *Memoirs* and attacked the behaviour of notable figures from the world of culture who, he maintained, could have expressed their condolences in a more sincere manner. He is said to have worn a black tie for the rest of his life in mourning for his late brother, the former attractive and healthy member of the 'Dioscuri', in contrast to himself, who had known so many years of illness but had somehow survived them.

Was de Chirico a joker, as Dr Bucarelli had thought? He shared Savinio's irony, even if his own did not always contain the poetic element that characterized everything the younger man wrote, but his reaction to his brother's death was proof that he could be serious, as he always was about his family. If he was not constantly a joker, however, de Chirico had long ago learned to play a part. At first he did so unconsciously, but by the time Cocteau wrote in 1928 about the theatrical quality of his work he himself was on the stage, observing as it were a stage within that stage, on which his metaphysical painting appeared as though by magic, like a performance enhanced with tricks of production. After years spent giving explanations, with the war over and his personal life more or less in order he now began to perform himself, attacking everyone else, from Breton and the surrealists to the critics and festival organizers of the 1950s and 1960s.

It was during the late 1950s that one English visitor, a young publisher at the time, remembers meeting him on several occasions. One thing in particular struck him: de Chirico was a character from *opera buffa*; he played his part, he entertained as though programmed to do so, he said all the perverse and contradictory things he was expected to say. He could even give the impression that his early painting was a joke like everything else; nothing was to be taken too seriously – the Italians did not care for that. The whole 'performance' was unreal, even if it was happening in reality, my friend reported. It was a visit to another world – a world of illusion, puzzling in its way but also stimulating, for here was the man who had painted all those controversial works, now scattered over the world and many of them worth vast sums of money. He had no intention of retiring.

It could be assumed that the metaphysical world had faded; de

Chirico may have thought he was no longer moving through a strange darkness, feeling his way. Which may be the reason why in 1950 the *Almanach surréaliste du demi-siècle*, published in Paris by André Breton, had reproduced a version of that early symbolic painting *The Child's Brain*: but in this version the eyes were open. Whose idea was it? Who did the retouching? If one mystery had been destroyed, another had been created. Most of the surrealists did not notice – and that was another kind of mystery, which amused Breton.

In the summer of 1962 the ongoing story of the de Chirico fakes reached London, making headlines in the *Daily Mail* and to a lesser extent in the *Daily Express*. '"Tate pictures are fakes," says painter'; '"Not my own Work," says Artist.' De Chirico claimed that he had known nothing about these so-called 'fakes' until 'friends returning from London recently told me that they had "loved my various paintings at the Tate"'. He had asked for photographs at once. Four works were on show: *The Painter's Family*, owned by the gallery, and three paintings on long-term loan from the collector Edward James, who was then living in the USA. The painter claimed that he had written to the Tate asking for these three works to be removed. He told the *Daily Mail* reporter who went to see him in Italy that he was 'the world's most copied painter' and that people copied him from revenge 'because I have so often denounced the various disorderly practices that go on in the art world today'. In Britain the painter John Piper, who had previously been a trustee of the Tate for seven years, was asked for his opinion. 'He was a wonderful painter before the war,' he said. 'But since then he has turned against all his early work.' The Deputy Keeper of the Tate Gallery, Norman Reid, reminded the *Daily Express* that this was not the first time that de Chirico had repudiated his early work.

The problem did not stop with the newspapers but reached the next Tate Gallery board meeting. According to the September minutes, the director, John Rothenstein, read a synopsis of the relevant correspondence and added that 'the position had now been further complicated by the claim of Mr Igor Markevitch to own one of the pictures in question [Markevitch had known de Chirico well in the

1920s]. There was a possibility that de Chirico might issue a writ against the Tate, ordering the withdrawal of the pictures from exhibition.' It was decided that both the artist and Mr Markevitch should be requested to write to Mr James. (After the latter's death in 1984 the collection he had assembled at West Dean in Sussex was dispersed and sold.)

For de Chirico the years passed with continued output of all kinds, including designs for further productions at La Scala, the Florence Maggio Musicale and elsewhere. But for others time had run out. In 1966 André Breton, one-time admirer and friend, but later enemy, died, aged seventy. The last few years of his life had been made more comfortable by the sale, which he had made with reluctance, of *The Child's Brain*, which had been so influential in the early days of surrealism, even while the movement was still in formation. De Chirico had never stopped attacking the surrealists, while the latter-day surrealists and their supporters had never stopped admiring and exhibiting and writing about the early de Chirico while ignoring anything he had painted after the early 1920s. However, he was to outlive nearly all of them. The surrealist associates Hans Arp and Alberto Giacometti died in the same year as Breton; Marcel Duchamp followed two years later. Francis Picabia had died in 1953; Yves Tanguy, who had been deeply impressed by the early de Chirico, in 1955. Oscar Dominguez and Wolfgang Paalen, both well-known names in the annals of surrealism, both committed suicide in the late 1950s. Nobody could have replaced André Breton as the *chef d'école*, but the movement did not fade into mere history: it survives actively as an attitude of mind, a way of life and an essential element in many new, or supposedly new, movements of today.

The English critic William Feaver maintained in 1982 that the surrealists 'loved de Chirico's clarity and the way he dragged sex into everything'. He never stopped doing so, even in later work, expressing it at different levels of consciousness and producing an orgasmic type of reaction from critics, who reacted with destructive anger often bordering on the sadistic. In 1996 the British artists Gilbert and George told Shere Hite, the psychosexual investigator, that they saw sex as 'the most important thing in art' and believed that 'the power of living is sex. There is nothing else.' Breton, who believed in the power of erotism, would have been interested in that, but what would de Chirico have made of it? His childhood, with his prudish father and domineering mother, had not brought him the capacity for easy sexual happiness. Raissa had even said that he used to visited a brothel once a week, until he felt she had 'purified' him (his words), although he was 'not worth much as a lover' (her words in 1978). It would amuse him in later life to respond to questions about sex in his usual paradoxical way. He is said to have once told a group of older women at the Caffè Greco in Rome what he felt about it, after they had asked him for an opinion. 'There's nothing more beautiful', he insisted, 'than not having intimate relations with the woman you love.' It sounded like a return to the courtly love of the Middle Ages. 'Then you don't see sex as part of love?' 'No,' replied de Chirico, adding that his brother, Savinio, had felt the same way. He also expressed a hope that someone would explain to him the meaning of 'sexual problems' – not 'sex', just 'sexual problems'. Raissa had said he was a great romantic, and there was a story about de Chirico falling in love with a beautiful woman in Rome: when he went to see her he would scatter laurel leaves along the stairs and landings on the way to her apartment. One day, when Raissa herself was obviously in a good mood, long after their separation, she told him when she happened to see him in Rome that if she had not been in love with him once already she would fall in love with him now.

In 1970 the first 'official' retrospective exhibition of de Chirico's work was organized at the Palazzo Reale in Milan by an international group of experts including Wieland Schmied from Hanover and David Sylvester from London. In March of that year de Chirico himself wrote an article in *L'Espresso* explaining his current activity. Recently, he said, he had returned to old themes for a new edition of *Calligrammes* (Apollinaire's collection of 'visual' poems, first published in 1918), and he referred to his current motif showing the sun (or even the moon) in a house, with a long black line resembling an electric cable linking it to the horizon. He had used a similar motif with zigzag rays in 1931 as part of the decor of Lifar's ballet *Bacchus et Ariane*. The painter also referred to the mysterious sea-bathing scenes he had worked on, which some critics have seen as comic, although Patrick Waldberg, historian of surrealism, could still find a 'subtle mystery' in these as well as in other later works, such as those featuring horses, archaeologists and gladiators, and suggested that de Chirico had not forgotten the 'myth-creating, angst-creating inspiration' of his earlier paintings. The artist himself, continuing his *L'Espresso* article, said, 'They are subjects which derive from reading or dreaming, simply subjects for working on, as used by writers or poets, revelations which come to me when I am about to fall asleep.' In 1971 he explained further, in *Vita* on 9 October. Sometimes he would look at one of his earlier paintings and see how it could be improved or at least rearranged. Some of the '*bagni misteriosi*' subjects came to him when he was half-dreaming, he said.

In January 1972 he was already eighty-three, but that did not prevent him from visiting the USA for a show entitled 'De Chirico by de Chirico' at the New York Cultural Center. An interview by David L. Shirey for the *New York Times* (21 January) appeared under the headline 'Paradoxical Chirico here for Show'. The journalist thought de Chirico looked the part of *Pictor Optimus*: 'An authoritarian bulk of a man with white hair, an aquiline nose and the general appearance of a 19th century Italian statesman'. Everything de Chirico said was true to form. There were about 150 works on view, mostly from his own collection, and he declared proudly that every one of them was authentic, whereas most de Chirico exhibitions included a proportion of fakes. He thought there were at least 3,000 forgeries in existence – some in very good collections. He found it strange that even some of his seventy or so self-portraits had been forged. (His only competitor in the self-portrait field was the German Max Beckmann.) De Chirico knew that he had been accused of copying, forging or predating his own work, but he maintained that if he used any theme from the past it was 'not a repetition but a variation'. He acted his part to the very end: in New York he had seen no exhibition except his own, he said, and he admitted that he liked the city best from the air – 'I can't see modern art from up there.' He then went home, while the exhibition moved on to the National Gallery of Canada in Toronto, where it did not fare too well.

It was the first major retrospective of works by de Chirico to appear in Canada, but it did not please the *Toronto Star*. On 24 June 1972 Wayne Edmondstone made his reaction devastatingly clear: 'For the past fifty years, de Chirico's output has generally been regarded as, in the words of one critic [whom he does not name], "the work of a self-plagiarizing bore".' The Toronto critic nevertheless found the show relevant 'if for no other reason than it provides a detailed record of the maestro's decline'. Edmondstone had obviously been reading past assessments of the painter's work and presumably agreed with them: this painting was 'an archaeology of the self' – that is, 'the reacting of childhood images, impressions and experiences in a unique way, which gives them an artistic life of their own'. So far, so good; but the later work was apparently the excavation of 'a territory where very little of value was ever really buried'. There were, for example, garish plugged-in suns (with plugged-in shadows). Edmondstone decided that these works reached 'depths of self-parody undreamed of even by Dalí'. Unfortunately for the painter's reputation, many people would agree with this, even if art critics are perpetually fascinated by the origins of de Chirico's imagery.

The English translation of de Chirico's *Memoirs* had appeared late in 1971, to much disapproval: 'spiteful ridicule of the Surrealist group'; 'repetitive and petty vituperation . . . deplorable reading . . . inane reminiscences . . .' Yet M. A. Ford, writing in the *Arts Review* of 29 January 1972, was much more understanding. The *Memoirs* were seen as 'most invigorating' and, despite the artist's 'blatant egotism', they contained 'a *Tristram Shandy* quality of innocence . . . quirky idiosyncrasies . . . the enjoyment of wandering off at a tangent from the subject; the striking, off-beat particularities of human behaviour'. Although 'surrealist' was 'a dirty word in de Chirico's vocabulary', there was something of surrealism in 'his way of recording his life, and what he sees, of throwing everyday things and events into unfamiliar juxtaposition, or even more, into a prominence which is not normally their due. This is essential "Surrealism".' The reviewer ended with a reference to the words of Eric Newton about the 1949 London exhibition: de Chirico was not inaugurating a new 'ism': he was making 'an attempt to revive an old one – Humanism – and to protest against the non-Humanistic art with which so many twentieth-century painters have been experimenting'.

Four years after his first 'official' retrospective, in Milan, there came another sign that the grand old man was now classed as respectable. In November 1974, when he was eighty-six, de Chirico was elected as *associé étranger* to the Académie des Beaux-Arts de l'Institut de France, taking the place of the Lithuanian-born sculptor Jacques Lipchitz who had died the previous year. He must surely have been gratified, for his hard words about the French might well have led them to decide that they did not want to have him among their associates. He had covered pages of his *Memoirs* with complaints about the French and their slavish imitation by the Italians, and he had once been so rude about them in a newspaper interview that the French ambassador in Italy had apparently protested. However, they seemed to have forgiven him.

At his reception he did not deliver a long speech in honour of his predecessor, as many new associates did at this part of the ceremony; he merely referred to Lipchitz as 'that noble artist' whose 'very personal and powerful work is known both in France and throughout the world'. Speaking of himself, he said, 'I shall do everything I can to be worthy of this election. I shall try to perfect my art by endowing it with more depth and perfecting its form, the basis of all true painting.' All he said was predictable: 'I wish to add that I have never belonged to any artistic movement and that my principal concern has always been to paint well.'

He remembered that it was in Paris, in 1912, where he had first exhibited his work and where in 1913 he had first sold a painting. He added his personal credo:

> I believe that the role of the artist in society consists first of all in the execution of his work; it is precisely in achieving this conception that the artist should do everything possible for his work to attain even

more perfection, which from a philosophical point of view is Utopia; but the pursuit of this aim leads the creator constantly to achieve greater things.

He had, he said, remained faithful to these principles, and finally, in a single sentence, he summarized his entire working life: 'independent of any school, following my path in the midst of adverse currents, unconcerned with fashion and faithful to the great courage praised by our great Delacroix, who wrote in his journal: "To show courage when your past is threatened is the greatest sign of strength."'

Monsieur Charles Kunstler, President of the Académie des Beaux-Arts at this date, an industrious polygraph of eighty-seven, traced de Chirico's career in detail. He mentioned the style and content of the painting through its various phases, referring to 1928 as the 'year of struggle, the year of Breton's *Surrealism and Painting*', which praised the early work but 'condemned without mercy your later productions'. He ventured a few reactions to the painting and made a special mention of the *Self-Portrait* in sixteenth-century costume, dating from 1959, 'with your right hand on your hip and your left holding a sword. Rembrandt had done the same in Amsterdam three centuries ago. He had painted a masterpiece. So did you.'

Near the end of his speech the President referred to the philosophical and poetic side of de Chirico's nature. He mentioned a few lines the painter had written in 1968 on the back of his *Oedipus and the Sphinx*:

> Might life not be one vast lie?
> Might it be only the shadow of a fleeting dream?
> Might it not be only the echo of mysterious
> blows struck against the mountain rocks where no one
> apparently has seen the other side?

The President closed with a reference to a 'delightful' painting, rare among de Chirico's work, for it was entitled *Apparition of Roses* and depicted three rosebuds. Beneath the preparatory drawing for this painting the artist had written, 'In my dreams, these roses suddenly appeared like a surprising decor revealed by the rise of a curtain.' 'Do not be upset,' said Monsieur Kunstler, 'dear, great, very great artist, if I tell you that in those roses, so attractive and so beautiful, I like to see the uniting of nature, the metaphysical spirit and poetic reality.' The painting that caused this lyrical moment has not been traced but may possibly have been similar to the *Red Roses* of 1920–1, although the flowers in that could not be described as buds.

The photograph of the new *associé étranger*, in his academic dress, shows a white-haired gentleman with an attractively cheerful half-smile – totally different from all those perplexed, even melancholy, self-portraits he had painted during the previous sixty years. He no doubt felt he deserved this election, even if it meant a reconciliation with France. The following year he accepted a high honour from Germany. The journalist Madeleine Chapsal had wondered, when she interviewed André Breton in 1962, if the once subversive surrealist leader had ever dreamed of such official success. If it had been offered, he would surely have refused it.

What now for de Chirico? Would he gracefully accept retirement? Would there be no more painting, no more complacent or aggressive newspaper articles, no more exhibitions? Far from it.

In 1975 I went to Wildenstein's gallery in London's West End to see a travelling exhibition of de Chirico's work that had already been shown in France and elsewhere. Over forty of the paintings, water-colours, gouaches and sculptures were dated after 1970, including the 1975 *Enigma of the Greek Remains*, which is thought to have been one of the last works the painter completed. There were echoes from the past: endless remakes of piazzas and mannequins, as well as horses, warriors, still lifes, mysterious baths. In fact the whole de Chirico land-scape was there, provided the visitor and potential buyer did not demand early authentic metaphysical exteriors. The selection of work seemed to prove that de Chirico was ready to give collectors what they thought they wanted: he was ready to reproduce, with varying degrees of imitation, any theme from the past. But one critic insisted that these were no slavish copies: each 'adaptation' included minute and intriguing differences of detail. Another wrote that de Chirico had invented all these motifs; they were his property, and he could surely use and reuse them as he wished. But apparently the collectors did not want any of these works, for nothing was sold.

Just as it may have seemed odd to think of de Chirico in the Académie des Beaux-Arts, it was as strange to find the catalogue for this London show introduced by the surrealist painter Félix Labisse, but he, too, was a member of the Académie. Surrealism seemed to have become respectable. Labisse wrote of de Chirico in suitably dramatic terms: 'In the involuntary role of incendiary he was the agent who touched off the explosive charge of Surrealism.' He then gave a brief description of the painter's revelation inspired by classical painting and of the lonely, mysterious path he now followed. Labisse insisted that de Chirico 'never burnt the bridges with his past nor broke faith with himself' – after all, the artist himself had said more than once that he had always followed the metaphysical style, even if he did so in unexpected ways.

Labisse summed up the personality and career of this energetic, near-inexplicable man – explicable only through his visual and written work. He began his piece by quoting a sentence from *Hebdomeros* – 'The essential task is to discover' – and ended it by a brief, memorable reference to de Chirico's 'tenacity . . . his refusal to conform, his disregard for convention, his appetite for the unusual and the unknown, and his instinctive feeling for quality, [which] have established him as the great Solitary of modern painting'. De Chirico's researches into technique and the 'quality' of materials are well known, but not everyone would agree about the 'quality' of some of his paintings.

The exhibition at Wildenstein's was, as far as is known, the last one-man show of de Chirico's work held in Britain during his lifetime, but a dozen or so early works were included in 'Dada and Surrealism Reviewed' at the Hayward Gallery in London at the beginning of 1978.

He was never out of the news for long. In 1977 developments in the long story about fakes and forgeries of his work had reached the *The Times* in London. A magistrate in Florence had discovered a whole art factory in the town. Over a thousand paintings had been cleverly produced – ninety of them reputedly by de Chirico, and others by well-known twentieth-century Italians including Renato Guttuso, Filippo de Pisis and Giorgio Morandi. The factory was in the apartment of a local painter, where there were even more incriminating discoveries, including a notary's seal, obviously stolen, and other equipment clearly intended for use in forging signatures. The magistrate issued six arrest warrants and seventeen summonses, two of them against Milan art dealers who had been acting as official art experts in the law courts.

The factory's activities were thought to have been going on for fifteen years or so, and seemed to prove that de Chirico's complaints and lawsuits were not merely an aspect of his eccentricity or his persecution complex or, as the Italian press sometimes dared to allege, his chosen method of stirring up controversy and causing the price of his work – the genuine work – to rise. He had vowed to 'catch these dogs one day and make them eat their brushes and paint'; with the help of others he seemed to have succeeded. But there was no end to the controversy, and in at least one case he was forced to recompense a gallery owner whom he had accused of dishonest dealing.

The year 1978 was a bad one for Italy. The Red Brigades kidnapped and murdered the Prime Minister, Aldo Moro, and terrorist activity continued later in the year even after some members of the Brigades had been convicted and sentenced for various crimes. Mount Etna, in Sicily, began to erupt unexpectedly. And on 20 November, four months after his ninetieth birthday, Giorgio de Chirico died.

He was buried in the church of San Francesco a Ripa at Trastevere, just outside Rome. His tomb is none too easy to find: it is located in a small room behind the first chapel on the left of the entrance door, built into the back wall. It is in striated white marble enclosed in a dark grey frame, and carries a short inscription:

GIORGIO DE CHIRICO
PICTOR OPTIMUS
A • 1888–1978 • Ω

Scholars and tourists come to this church to see one of Bernini's most famous baroque sculptures, the monument to the Blessed Ludovica Albertoni, ecstatic at the prospect of entering heaven as she expires on her deathbed. It is thought to date from about 1674. De Chirico's life could also be said to be something of a baroque creation, and in one way that life continued, for in the years immediately following his death all aspects of his work figured in many European exhibitions, covering a variety of themes: surrealism, realism, metaphysical art, modern Italian art, theatre art, fantastic art.

In 1980 there was a one-man show at the Hermitage museum in Leningrad, and two years later the Tate Gallery in London honoured him with an important exhibition which had been organized under the auspices of the International Council of the Museum of Modern Art in New York. It received wide and serious press coverage, but several critics wished that more of the controversial later work had been included. On the other hand, the visitor was able to see no fewer than eighteen versions of *The Disquieting Muses*, originally of 1917. That was disquieting indeed.

In the hope of redressing the balance, a show entitled 'Late de Chirico' was organized, or at least introduced, by Isabella Far in 1985 and was seen in Bristol, Oxford and Sheffield. It included some lively, even impressive, work, and visitors could be reminded of something the artist had written in his *Memoirs*: 'In addition to being a great painter and a great man, I also have a great mission to fulfil.'

There were two aspects to that mission: the first to prove himself *Pictor Optimus* for eternity; the second to destroy the belief that there was any value in 'modern art'. He convinced at least himself that he had succeeded. But did he or anyone else solve the enigma of his personality, the enigma of the solitary superman? 'One could write endless epilogues about the history and psychological origins of the enigma,' wrote the historian of the *aenigma* Marcel Bernasconi in 1964, 'without succeeding in explaining in any certain and precise fashion the profound reasons for the passion it has always aroused; these reasons are as profound as the enigma itself; a passion explained is a passion no longer.' One thing is certain: de Chirico's work occupies a well-deserved place somewhere between the *Invented Prisons* of the eighteenth-century Piranesi and the *Invisible Cities* of Italo Calvino published in 1972.

Where is de Chirico's place in twentieth-century painting, and how does he stand *vis-à-vis* surrealism, two decades after his death? When the influential period of his metaphysical painting was over he tended to take up contradictory attitudes: he would either dismiss his early work as unimportant (but still fit for copying) or else claim that he had never given up metaphysical painting. He outlived André Breton and the 'official' surrealist movement, but he and his work remain linked to surrealism by the juxtaposition of disparate elements ranging from Greek mythology to German philosophy, which were always in his conscious mind, and the sexual symbolism of which, according to Breton, he remained unconscious.

There is no simple explanation of his behaviour or his attitudes – that 'enigma' of his personality, which in the end he unconsciously preferred not to solve and in fact complicated still further – but his whole career, his many changes of style and his still undervalued writing have made him arguably one of the most baffling and the most memorable of the first and last super-realists.

Notes and Sources

Where possible, sources and some explanatory details are indicated briefly in the text, while details of books, periodicals, catalogues, etc. not given in full here are provided in the bibliography.

The following five works are essential for consultation:

- Maurizio Fagiolo dell'Arco, *L'Opera completa di de Chirico 1908–1924* (Rizzoli, Milan, 1984). This contains biographical details, reproductions, with notes, of most works painted before 1924 and several writings by the artist, with lists of others and many extracts from contemporary critics.

- Maurizio Calvesi and Gioia Mori, *De Chirico* (Art e Dossier; Giunti, Florence, 1988). Critical articles, colour reproductions and chronology.

- Giorgio de Chirico, *Memorie della mia vita* (Astrolabio, Rome, 1945; 2nd edn (expanded with coverage of 1945–60) Rizzoli, Milan, 1962); translated by Margaret Crosland as *Memoirs of Giorgio de Chirico* (Peter Owen, London, 1971), to which page numbers refer. Selective and controversial.

- James Thrall Soby, *Giorgio de Chirico* (Museum of Modern Art, New York, 1955). This is an important revised version of the author's *The Early Chirico* (Dodd, Mead, New York, 1941), including many plates, both colour and black and white, and two appendices giving translations of writings by de Chirico from his first period in Paris, 1911–15. It deals only briefly with the later work, 1925–8.

- Pia Vivarelli (ed.), *Giorgio de Chirico*, introduced by Giorgio de Marchis (2 vols, Galleria Nazionale d'Arte Moderna, Rome, 1981). This catalogue, compiled for an exhibition in Rome from 11 November 1981 to 3 January 1982, contains a complete list of the exhibitions in which de Chirico participated until that date, a select list of his own writings and a bibliography of books and articles written about him. It also contains specialist articles about various aspects of his work.

Introduction

For Cocteau's *The Lay Mystery* (*Le Mystère laïc*), see Cocteau's *My Contemporaries* (Peter Owen, London, 1967, edited by Margaret Crosland), pp. 101–27 and the bibliography below.

Orwell originally wrote 'Benefit of Clergy: Some Notes on Salvador Dalí' for the *Saturday Book* in 1944, but it was 'suppressed on grounds of obscenity' and not published until 1946, when it was included in his *Critical Essays* (Secker and Warburg, London). John Sturrock's *The Language of Autobiography: Studies in the First Person Singular* was published by Cambridge University Press, Cambridge, in 1997.

Benvenuto Cellini (1500–71): sculptor, goldsmith and engraver. His *Vita* was first published in 1728, long after he wrote or dictated it; English versions include *Autobiography*, trans. George Bull (Penguin, Harmondsworth, 1969).

Vittorio Alfieri (1749–1803): poet. He completed his *Vita* shortly before his death; an anonymous English translation appeared in 1810 and was revised by E. R. Vincent as *Memoirs* (Oxford University Press, Oxford, 1961).

Chapter 1: The Child's Brain

See de Chirico, *Memoirs*, pp. 13–52; Cocteau, *The Lay Mystery*; Luisa Spagnoli, *Lunga vita di Giorgio de Chirico*; Alberto Savinio, *Casa 'La Vita'*.

André Breton (1896–1951): future leader of the surrealists.

Savinio on the origins of the de Chirico family: letter to *Il Meridiano di Roma*; November 1937; see Calvesi and Mori, *De Chirico*, p. 45.

Chapter 2: Paraphrase on the Finding of a Glove

De Chirico, *Memoirs*; Soby, *Giorgio de Chirico*; Savinio, *Casa 'La Vita'*.

De Chirico, 'On Metaphysical Art': *Valori Plastici*, April–May 1919; see translation by Gillian Tisdall in Carrà et al., *Metaphysical Art*.

'Modern painting and Nazism': de Chirico *Memoirs*, p. 57.

Friedrich, 'Close your bodily eye . . .': quoted in Sorrell, *The Duality of Vision: Genius and Universality in the Arts*.

Arnold Böcklin (1827–1901): Swiss-born painter specializing in mythological subjects. Some of his symbolist-style work later influenced the surrealists. See also Jullian, *Dreamers of Decadence*.

De Chirico on Böcklin: *Il Convegno* (Milan), May 1920.

Max Klinger (1857–1920): German painter, sculptor and graphic artist. His *Paraphrase on the Finding of a Glove* (1881) was highly successful.

De Chirico on Klinger: *Il Convegno* (Milan), 20 November 1921.

Alfred Kubin (1877–1959): Austrian artist and illustrator. His novel *Die Andere Seite* (translated by Denver Lindley as *The Other Side* (Gollancz, London, 1969)) was originally published in 1909, his *Autobiography* being added to the second edition.

Otto Weininger (1880–1903): Austrian thinker.

Paul Eluard (1895–1952): leading surrealist poet, 1919–38; joined the Communist Party then, later, became well-known Resistance writer.

De Chirico on the effects of reading Nietzsche: see Soby, *Giorgio de Chirico*, Appendices A and B.

Filippo Tommaso Marinetti (1876–1944): Italian poet and novelist; founder of the futurist movement.

For Guillaume Apollinaire (1880–1918), see Chapter 3.

Chapter 3: 'A City Full of Life, Movement, Intelligent People'

De Chirico, *Memoirs*; Shattuck, *The Banquet Years*; Savinio, *Casa 'La Vita'*; Spagnoli, *Lunga vita di Giorgio de Chirico*.

Schopenhauer on statues: quoted by de Chirico in 'On Metaphysical Art'.

Anatole France (1884–1924): prolific writer of literary and historical works and many novels. Awarded the Nobel Prize in 1921. Despite his adhesion to socialist ideas late in life the surrealists attacked him.

Alfred Jarry (1873–1907): his farce *Ubu Roi*, which caused a scandal in 1876, has been seen as a precursor of surrealism and the theatre of the absurd.

Henri (Douanier) Rousseau (1844–1910): influential 'primitive' painter.

Arnold Bennett (1867–1931): successful English novelist, living mainly in Paris between 1902 and 1912. See the entries for 31 January and 8 July 1911 in *The Journals of Arnold Bennett*, selected and edited by Frank Swinnerton (Penguin, Harmondsworth, 1954).

For details of Savinio's life and publications, see his *Hermaphrodito e altri romanzi*.

Pierre Laprade (1875–1931): successful French painter, much of his work being in the style of *fêtes galantes*.

Giovanni Papini (1881–1956): prolific writer, critic and editor; founder (with Ardengo Soffici) of the review *Lacerba*, 1913–15. Famous for his style of harsh critical review known as *stroncatura* and his polemical attitudes. Influenced by his conversion to Catholicism in 1920; later a Fascist. See also Calvesi's essay 'Da metafisico a psicofisico' in Calvesi and Mori, *De Chirico*.

Dino Campana (1885–1932): poet; influenced by Rimbaud (and his wandering life also prompted comparisons with the French poet) and by Nietzsche's *The Birth of Tragedy*. His mental instability limited his creative life, and he spent many years in mental hospitals.

Gabriele d'Annunzio (1863–1938): poet, playwright and novelist.

Calvesi on d'Annunzio: Calvesi and Mori, *De Chirico*, pp. 5–6.

Umberto Boccioni (1882–1916): Italian futurist painter and sculptor.

Paul Valéry (1871–1945): influential poet and critic.

Gustave Moreau (1826–98): painter and teacher, influential symbolist given to exotic and dramatic subjects.

André Gide (1869–1951): successful and controversial writer in most genres, winning the Nobel Prize in 1947.

Marie Laurencin (1885–1956): painter, best known for her poetic treatment of feminine subjects.

Les Soirées de Paris, edited by Apollinaire, quoted in Fagiolo dell'Arco, *L'Opera completa di de Chirico 1908–1924*, pp. 68–71.

Dunoyer de Segonzac (1884–1974): landscape painter and illustrator.

Luc-Albert Moreau (1882–1948): successful if undistinguished French painter.

Valori Plastici: Italian literary review edited by Mario Broglio (1891–1948) from 1918 to 1921; Savinio's article on his brother is translated in Carrà et al., *Metaphysical Art*.

Savinio on his music: *Les Soirées de Paris*, no. 23, 15 April 1914.

Chapter 4: The Enigma of Fatality

De Chirico, *Memoirs*; his war experiences are told on pp. 68–86.

Charles Péguy (1873–1914): prolific writer, founder in 1900 of the polemical journal *Cahiers de la quinzaine*; best remembered for his poetic drama *Jeanne d'Arc* (1897), his support for Alfred Dreyfus, his humanitarian socialism and his deep patriotism.

Alain-Fournier (Henri-Alban Fournier, 1886–1914): in addition to his great novel *Le Grand Meaulnes* (1913), his (posthumous) publications included two volumes of *Correspondance* with the critic Jacques Rivière (1948) and some short stories and prose poems; he also left an unfinished novel.

Apollinaire's wartime experiences and writing: see Pascal Pia, *Apollinaire par lui-même* (Seuil, Paris, 1954).

Gide's journal dated 12 August 1914, quoted in Margaret Crosland, *Jean Cocteau* (Peter Nevill, London, 1955), pp. 39–40.

Picasso on camouflage: see Janet Hobhouse, *Everybody Who Was Anybody: A Biography of Gertrude Stein* (Weidenfeld and Nicolson, London, 1975), p. 105.

Ungaretti and de Chirico's Paris studio: see Fagiolo dell'Arco, *L'Opera completa di de Chirico 1908–1924*, p. 70.

Giuseppe Ungaretti (1888–1970): Italian poet, born in Egypt; educated in Paris and influenced by Apollinaire. Worked as a journalist, taught in Brazil from 1936 to 1942 and became a professor of Italian literature in Rome in 1962.

Jean Paulhan (1884–1968): influential French literary critic, long associated with *Nouvelle revue française* and co-founder of *Les Lettres françaises* during the

German occupation of France. Became a member of the Académie française in 1964.

Philippe Soupault (1897–19): poet, co-founder with Breton and Aragon of *Littérature* (first series, 1911–21) and collaborator with Breton on *The Magnetic Fields* (1919).

Louis Aragon (1897–1983): novelist, poet and political activist; co-founder with Breton and Soupault of *Littérature* in 1919 and signatory of the Surrealist Manifesto. Converted to Communism after a visit to the USSR.

For Apollinaire's *Lettre-Océan*, see Shattuck, *The Innocent Eye*, pp. 240–62.

For the Gartzen portrait, see Vivarelli, *Giorgio de Chirico*, vol. 1, pp. 62–3.

Romain Rolland (1866–1944): writer and musicologist; awarded the Nobel Prize in 1915.

Henri Barbusse (1873–1935): novelist and journalist; his Goncourt Prize novel of 1916, *Le Feu*, was published in English as *Under Fire: The Story of a Squad*, translated by Fitzwater Wray, introduced by Brian Rhys (J. M. Dent, London, 1917).

The 1995 edition of Savinio's *Hermaphrodito* gives details of his decision to give up music, pp. 50–1.

Filippo de Pisis (1886–1956): regarded as one of the 'metaphysical' painters when young, his style later became more impressionistic. The photograph of him with de Chirico is reproduced in many books on surrealism and in the catalogue of the exhibition *Le Surréalisme 1922–1942*, shown at the Musée des Arts Décoratifs, Paris, from 8 June to 24 September 1972. His article on de Chirico appeared on 11 October 1916 in *Gazzetta Ferrarese*; see Fagiolo dell'Arco, *L'Opera completa di de Chirico 1908–1924*, p. 71.

Tristan Tzara (1896–1963): Romanian-born French poet, founder of the Dada movement in Zurich, 1916.

Corrado Govoni (1884–1965): lyric poet and novelist.

De Chirico on his 'biscuit' paintings: Spagnoli, *Lunga vita di Giorgio de Chirico*, pp. 89–90.

De Chirico on Ferrara: *Il Convegno* (Milan), August 1920.

Gino Severini (1883–1966): painter taught first by the futurist Giacomo Balla but later impressed by the divisionist and neo-impressionist theories of Seurat; he became interested in mosaics and frescos, with which he decorated churches in Switzerland.

Savinio on Ferrara: *Hermaphrodito e altri romanzi*, p. 28.

The '*très bien*' woman: Spagnoli, *Lunga vita di Giorgio de Chirico*, p. 98.

For Il Seminario, see Spagnoli, *Lunga vita di Giorgio de Chirico*, and Vivarelli, *Giorgio de Chirico*. For Carlo Carrà, see Caroline Tisdall's historical foreword to Massimo Carrà et al., *Metaphysical Art*. Carlo Carrà's autobiography was *La mia vita* (Longanesi, Rome, 1943; 2nd edn, Rizzoli, Milan, 1945).

For de Chirico's first known letter to Carrà, see Vivarelli, *Giorgio de Chirico*, vol. 2, p. 16.

Tristan Tzara's review of de Chirico's painting: Fagiolo dell'Arco, *L'Opera completa di de Chirico 1908–1924*, p. 72.

Chapter 5: The Disquieting Muses

De Chirico's article on Apollinaire is quoted in Calvesi and Mori *De Chirico*, p. 17.

For de Chirico's participation in exhibitions in Rome and Paris at this period, see Vivarelli, *Giorgio de Chirico*, vol. 2, pp. 18–24, and de Chirico, *Memoirs*, p. 89.

Roberto Longhi (1890–1960): art historian and critic; an expert on Caravaggio, he later became Professor of Art History at the University of Florence.

De Chirico and Schopenhauer's poems: Vivarelli, *Giorgio de Chirico*, vol. 2, p. 11.

Early poems from Paris: Giorgio de Chirico, *Poésies, poèmes*, edited by Maurizio Fagiolo dell'Arco (Rome, 1980).

'*Viaggio e villeggiatura*' and '*Promontorio*': Fagiolo dell'Arco, *L'Opera completa di de Chirico 1908–1924*, pp. 71–2, 75.

Mario Broglio (1891–1948): founder of the review *Valori Plastici* (1918–21) and painter with metaphysical tendencies. *Valori Plastici* published six important pieces by de Chirico. See Carrà et al., *Metaphysical Art*.

De Chirico's review of Carrà's *Pittura metafisica*: Vivarelli, *Giorgio de Chirico*, vol. 2, p. 19.

Giorgio Morandi (1896–1964): metaphysical painter, born Bologna; he never worked in Paris.

The de Chirico bibliography in Vivarelli includes three pieces about Gustave Courbet (1819–77), the French realist whom he admired. The best known is the short booklet *Courbet* published by *Valori Plastici* in 1925 after the closure of the review.

'Revelation' at the Villa Borghese: de Chirico, *Memoirs*, pp. 96–7.

Life in Rome, 1919: de Chirico, *Memoirs*, and Spagnoli, *Lunga vita di Giorgio de Chirico*.

'An elderly woman painter . . .': Spagnoli, *Lunga vita di Giorgio de Chirico*, p. 104.

De Chirico on figs: *Hebdomeros*, translated by Crosland, p. 70.

Women in the *Memoirs*: Marie Laurencin, p. 66; Matilde Serao (1856–1927; journalist who wrote forty novels and founded and ran a newspaper, *Il Giorno*, in Naples), p. 74; Pasqualina Spadini and Isabella Far, p. 99; Braun sisters, p. 109.

Armando Spadini (1883–1925): originally worked in ceramics, went through a period of 'naturalist reaction' and was later regarded as an impressionist.

Emile Jaques-Dalcroze (1865–1950): Swiss composer whose system of musical education is known as 'Eurythmics'.

Marie Bashkirtseff (1860–84): Russian girl who lived in Paris; well known for the selections from her diary published in France in 1887, after her early death from tuberculosis, and translated into many languages (including English in 1890).

For a de Chirico caricature of 'Roch Grey' with Picasso, see Vivarelli, *Giorgio de Chirico*, vol. 2, p. 13.

Valentine de Saint-Point and the Marchesa Casati: Tisdall and Bossola, *Futurism*.

'The Return to the Craft': *Valori Plastici*, November–December 1920; see translation in Carrà et al., *Metaphysical Art*, pp. 141–6.

Massimo Bontempelli (1878–1960): novelist and critic, close to surrealism but preferring the term 'magical realism'.

Parade: an avant-garde ballet – a collaboration between Cocteau, Satie, Picasso and Massine – produced at the Châtelet Theatre, Paris, in May 1917; a famous flop.

Jacques Vaché (1896–1919): he impressed Breton with his 'Umour' and *désinvolture*, while the former surrealist José Pierre described him as the poet's 'Polar Star'. Breton was deeply upset by Vaché's unexpected death – either suicide or an accidental drugs overdose.

Breton on the 1922 de Chirico exhibition: Vivarelli, *Giorgio de Chirico*, vol. 2, p. 23.

René Magritte (1898–1923): influential surrealist painter. See '*La Ligne de vie*' in *Anthologie du surréalisme en Belgique*, edited by Christian Bussy (Gallimard, Paris, 1972), p. 389. Also Vivarelli, *Giorgio de Chirico*, vol. 2, p. 14.

Yves Tanguy (1900–55): joined the surrealists in 1925; his first sight of a de Chirico is described in Soby, *Giorgio de Chirico*, p. 151.

Raymond Radiguet (1903–23): adolescent prodigy, best known for *Le Diable au corps* (Grasset, Paris, 1923), published in English as *The Devil in the Flesh*, translated and introduced by Robert Baldick (Penguin, Harmondsworth, 1971).

De Chirico's March 1922 letter to Breton is translated in Soby, *Giorgio de Chirico*, pp. 158–9.

Max Ernst (1891–1976): German-born painter who came to Paris in 1919.

Emilio Cecchi (1884–1966): eminent if subjective critic of art and literature and art historian. See also Vivarelli, *Giorgio de Chirico*, vol. 2, p. 24.

Chapter 6: Salve Lutetia

'Fervent and haughty little book': Waldberg, *Surrealism*, p. 11.

The Dream of Tobias: see Vivarelli, *Giorgio de Chirico*, vol. 1, p. 76.

Paul Delvaux (1897–1994): Belgian surrealist painter.

Alfredo Casella (1883–1947): Italian composer who studied in Paris, producing work in most genres, including ballets. He anticipated the interest in the baroque, but his later work was mainly of neo-classical type.

Luigi Pirandello (1867–1936): prolific writer of fiction and drama; his best-known work is probably *Sei personaggi in cerca d'autore* (1920) (*Six Characters in Search of an Author*, trans. M. Musa in *Three Plays* (Penguin, London, 1995)). His theatrical company toured Europe after 1925. He was awarded the Nobel Prize for Literature in 1934.

Rolf de Maré: wealthy Swedish landowner who formed Les Ballets Suédois in 1924 with his compatriot Jean Börlin, who had had some training from Michel Fokine, as choreographer and leading dancer. Much of Börlin's work was controversial and not too popular, and the company was disbanded late in 1924.

Francis Picabia (1879–1953): editor of the review *291*, for which he designed many covers.

'Vale Lutetia' is reproduced in Fagiolo dell'Arco, *L'Opera completa di de Chirico 1908–1924*, pp. 76–7.

Stravinsky wrote *The Soldier's Tale* in 1918 after the revolution in Russia meant that neither he nor Diaghilev had any more funds. The *Tale* was to be 'read, acted and danced'; it was not expensive to stage and could be performed by a travelling company.

The details about Raissa Gurievitch Krol, de Chirico's first wife, are taken from Spagnoli, *Lunga vita di Giorgio de Chirico,* and from interviews with Raissa by C. Costantini (*Il Messaggero*, Rome, 13 October 1978) and C. Pilolli (*Gente*, Milan, 11 November 1978).

'Dominating Slav Jewess': note from de Chirico to the painter Pierre Roy; quoted in Calvesi and Mori, *De Chirico*, p. 38.

'Statues, Furniture and Generals' was written in French and published in Léonce Rosenberg's *Bulletin de l'effort moderne*, October 1927. For an English translation, see Carrà et al., *Metaphysical Art*.

Igor Markevitch (1912–83): *Etre et avoir été* was published by Gallimard, Paris, in 1980.

The surrealists insulted Anatole France in 1924, and during a banquet in celebration of the symbolist poet Saint-Pol Roux they caused so much disturbance that the police were called and the woman novelist and critic Rachilde was arrested. See Margaret Crosland, *Women of Iron and Velvet* (Constable, London 1976), p. 71.

Breton on de Chirico's copying: *Surrealism and Painting*, p. 17.

Unless otherwise indicated the source for the remainder of this chapter is Spagnoli, *Lunga vita di Giorgio de Chirico*. Owing to the author's untimely death in an accident, much of this information cannot be corroborated.

Queneau's review of the 1928 Brussels show: Calvesi and Mori, *De Chirico*, p. 39. Queneau, a surrealist in his youth, lived from 1903 to 1976.

In *Nadja* Breton wrote nearly three pages about de Chirico, expressing his regret, as usual, that the painter was not prepared to collaborate with the surrealists, but the passage is too long for quotation.

Sachs on Cocteau: Maurice Sachs, *Le Sabbat: Souvenirs d'une jeunesse orageuse* (Corrêa, Paris, 1946), p. 128. Maurice Sachs (1909–44), the grandson of Proust's friend Madame Strauss, was given to falling in love with writers, including Gide and Cocteau. He began to study for the priesthood but lost his vocation, lived by dishonest means and became a black marketeer during the German occupation of France. He wrote well, and one of his best-known books was *La Décade de l'illusion* (Gallimard, Paris, 1950). He later wrote to Cocteau repenting of his unkind remarks about him.

Vittorio Rieti (1898–1994): Italian composer, born in Egypt, becoming a US citizen in 1944. He studied composition with Respighi and Malipiero in Rome, lived in Paris from 1925 and left France for the USA in 1944. His many compositions include seventeen ballets and seven operas, in addition to symphonies, concertos, chamber music and songs.

For *Le Bal*, see the works by Richard Buckle, S. L. Grigoriev and Boris Kochno listed in the bibliography.

The ending of *Hebdomeros* is taken from p. 127 of the English translation.

Léonor Fini (1908–96): surrealist painter and designer of decors for many films and operas.

Chapter 7: The 'Most Profoundly Intelligent Person'

For personal life and Isabella Pakszwer, later de Chirico, see Spagnoli, *Lunga vita di Giorgio de Chirico*; see also *Il Messaggero* (Rome), 13 October 1978, and *Gente* (Milan), 11 and 18 November 1978.

Isabella's threat to kill herself: Spagnoli, *Lunga vita di Giorgio de Chirico*, pp. 137–8.

'The most profoundly intelligent person': de Chirico, *Memoirs*, p. 124.

Lifar on *Bacchus et Ariane*: Serge Lifar, *La Danse: La Danse académique et l'art chorégraphique* (Bibliothèque Méditations Editions Gonthier, Paris, 1965); see also his *Ma vie* (Julliard, Paris, 1965; translated with same title by James Holman Mason, Hutchinson, London, 1970).

I Puritani: de Chirico, *Memoirs*, p. 126; Vivarelli, *Giorgio de Chirico*, vol. 2, p. 33.

Mario Sironi (1885–1961): influenced by divisionism and futurism, his quasi-metaphysical painting was described by Caroline Tisdall (in Carrà et al., *Metaphysical Painting*) as containing 'violent emotions, dramatic forms, order and disorder mingled in a whirlwind of volumes and tones'.

Massimo Campigli (1895–1971): Florentine painter who worked mainly in Rome; influenced by the cubists but more profoundly by ancient Etruscan and Roman painting.

Achille Funi (1890–1972): associated with the futurists at first; later influenced by de Chirico and the surrealists.

Letter to Mussolini: State Archives, Ministry of Public Education; quoted on www.comune.roma.it/gal_com/storia/schedadechirico.html.

Sale of *Il Combattimento di Gladiatori*: Internet (as above).

Breton's complaint about the Italian flag: Polizzotti, *Revolution of the Mind*, p. 432.

Visit to the USA: de Chirico, *Memoirs*, pp. 130–1; Vivarelli, *Giorgio de Chirico*, vol. 2, pp. 34, 35 (three illustrations), 36.

Scheiner window display: *L'Illustrazione Italiana*, 13 February 1938; see Vivarelli, *Giorgio de Chirico*, vol. 2, pp. 34–6.

Death of de Chirico's mother: de Chirico, *Memoirs*, p. 135.

Savinio's 'My Mother Doesn't Understand Me': see his *Casa 'La Vita'* and de Chirico, *Memoirs*, p. 220.

De Chirico's *L'Illustrazione Italiana* piece on America: Vivarelli, *Giorgio de Chirico*, vol. 2, pp. 34–6.

Savinio's November 1937 letter to *Il Meridiano di Roma*: Calvesi and Mori, *De Chirico*, p. 45.

'Impact of Machines' show at the London Gallery: Vivarelli, *Giorgio de Chirico*, vol. 2, p. 37.

July 1938 Lefevre show: de Chirico, *Memoirs*, p. 140–1; Vivarelli, *Giorgio de Chirico*, vol. 2, p. 37.

De Chirico on London: *Memoirs*, p. 140.

'Sensitiveness': *Horizon*, vol. X, no. 55 (1944).

For the writings of Isabella Far (de Chirico), see de Chirico, *Memoirs*, p. 158, 159.

Chapter 8: Et Quid Amabo Nisi Quod Rerum Metaphysica Est?

The title, which translates as 'And what shall I love except the metaphysical?', is taken from the *Self-portrait* of 1920, now in the Staatsgalerie Moderne Kunst, Munich.

Estimated number of works by de Chirico: Vivarelli, *Giorgio de Chirico*, vol. 1, introduced by G. de Marchis, p. 9.

'Twelve periods' of de Chirico's paintings: Fagiolo dell'Arco, *L'Opera completa di de Chirico 1908–1924*, p. 6.

Palma Bucarelli: *L'Indipendente*, 12 May 1945; quoted in Vivarelli, *Giorgio de Chirico*, vol. 2, pp. 43–4, and in Calvesi and Mori, *De Chirico*, p. 46.

'Fakes' at the Galerie Allard: Vivarelli, *Giorgio de Chirico*, vol. 2, p. 44.

Categories of 'fakes': Spagnoli, *Lunga vita di Giorgio de Chirico*, p. 17.

The *Il Merlo Giallo* article by de Chirico appeared on 12 July 1948 and is quoted in Vivarelli, *Giorgio de Chirico*, vol. 2, p. 45.

Death of Savinio: chronology in his *Hermaphrodito e altri romanzi*, edited by

Tinterri, p. lxvii; de Chirico, *Memoirs*, pp. 200–9, 210, 217, 220–1.

The *Daily Mail* and *Daily Express* articles both appeared on 19 July 1962; the remarks by John Piper were in the first of these and by Norman Reid in the second.

William Feaver on de Chirico: *Observer*, 8 August 1982.

Gilbert and George on sex and art: *Guardian Weekend*, 25 October 1997.

Raissa on de Chirico as a lover: *Gente* (Milan), 11 November 1978.

De Chirico on sex: Spagnoli, *Lunga vita di Giorgio de Chirico*, p. 169.

The *L'Espresso* article is quoted in Vivarelli, *Giorgio de Chirico*, vol. 2, p. 51.

Patrick Waldberg on de Chirico: Carrà et al., *Metaphysical Art* (1971), p. 179.

Bibliography

Works by de Chirico

Courbet (Valori Plastici, Rome, 1925)

Hebdomeros: le peintre et son génie chez l'écrivain (Collection Bifur; Editions du Carrefour, Paris, 1929); reprinted in the Collection de l'Age d'Or series (Flammarion, Paris, 1964); translated by Margaret Crosland as *Hebdomeros: A Novel* (Peter Owen, London, 1964)

Memorie della mia vita (Astrolabio, Rome, 1945; Rizzoli, Milan, 1962); translated by Margaret Crosland as *Memoirs of Giorgio de Chirico* (Peter Owen, London, 1971)

For lists of selected articles published by de Chirico, see the books by Maurizio Fagiolo dell'Arco, James Thrall Soby and the catalogue edited by P. Vivarelli. See also translations by Caroline Tisdall in Carrà et al., *Metaphysical Art*.

Works about de Chirico

Calvesi, Maurizio and Gioia Mori, *De Chirico* (Art e Dossier; Giunti, Florence, 1988)

Carlino, Marcello, *Una penna per il pennello: Giorgio de Chirico scrittore* (Officino Edizione, Rome, 1989)

Cocteau, Jean, *Le Mystère laïc: essai d'étude indirecte* (Editions des Quatre Chemins, Paris, 1928; later included in vol. 1 of *Poésie critique* (Gallimard, Paris, 1959)

Faerna, José Maria (ed.), *De Chirico*, translated from the Spanish by Diane Cobos (Abrams, New York, 1995)

Fagiolo dell'Arco, Maurizio, *L'Opera completa di de Chirico 1908–1924* (Milan, 1984)

George, Waldemar, *Chirico, avec des fragments littéraires de l'artiste* (Chronique du Jour, Paris, 1928)

Soby, James Thrall, *Giorgio de Chirico* (Museum of Modern Art, New York, 1955)

Spagnoli, Luisa, *Lunga vita di Giorgio de Chirico* (Longanesi, Milan, 1971); a lively picture of de Chirico the joker but not for the serious student

Vitrac, Roger, *Georges di Chirico* (Les Peintres Français Nouveaux No. 29; Gallimard, Paris, 1927)

Vivarelli, P. (ed.), *Giorgio de Chirico* (2 vols, Galleria Nazionale d'Arte Moderna, Rome, 1981)

General works

Balakian, Anna, *Surrealism: The Road to the Absolute* (Noonday Press, New York, 1959)

Bennett, Arnold, *The Journals of Arnold Bennett*, selected and edited by Frank Swinnerton (Penguin, Harmondsworth, 1954)

Bernasconi, Marcel, *Histoire des énigmes* (Presses Universitaires de France, Paris, 1964)

Breton, André, *Anthologie de l'humour noir* (Jean-Jacques Pauvert, Paris, 1939; later editions 1947, 1966); *Entretiens (1913–1952)*, avec André Parinaud, etc. (Le Point du Jour; Gallimard, Paris, 1952; later edition 1969); *Manifestoes of Surrealism* (1924–42), translated by R. Seaver and H. R. Lane (Michigan University Press, Ann Arbor, 1972); *Nadja* (Gallimard, Paris, 1928); *Surrealism and Painting* (1928), translated by Simon Watson-Taylor (Macdonald, London, 1965)

Brion, Marcel, *L'Art fantastique* (Albin Michel, Paris, 1961)

Buckle, Richard, *Diaghilev* (Weidenfeld and Nicolson, London, 1979)

Caillois, Roger, *Au cœur du fantastique* (Gallimard, Paris, 1965)

Carrà, Massimo, Patrick Waldberg and Ewald Rathke, *Metaphysical Art*, historical foreword by Caroline Tisdall (Thames and Hudson, London, 1971)

Chamberlain, Lesley, *Nietzsche in Turin: The End of the Future* (Quartet, London, 1996)

Chapsal, Madeleine, *Envoyez la petite musique* (Grasset, Paris, 1984; formerly published as *Les Ecrivains en personne* (Julliard, Paris, 1960). For André Breton, see pp. 216–25; for Tristan Tzara, see pp. 286–9.

Dalí, Salvador, *The Secret Life of Salvador Dalí* (Vision Press, London, 1942)

Gibson, Michael, *Symbolism* (Taschen, London, 1996)

Gide, André, *Journals 1889–1949*, translated, selected and edited by Justin O'Brien (Penguin, Harmondsworth, 1967)

Grigoriev, S. L., *The Diaghilev Ballet 1909–1929* (Constable, London, 1953)

Grigson, Geoffrey, 'Courbet, Chirico and Constable' in *The Harp of Aeolus and Other Essays on Art, Literature and Nature* (Routledge, London, 1948), pp. 135, 149–50

Jullian, Philippe, *Dreamers of Decadence*, translated by Robert Baldick (Phaidon, London, 2nd edn 1974)

Kochno, Boris, *Diaghilev and the Ballets Russes* (Allen Lane, London, 1971)

Mann, Carol, *Paris: Artistic Life in the Twenties and Thirties* (Laurence King, London, 1996)

Markevitch, Igor, *Etre et avoir été* (Gallimard, Paris, 1980)

Muselli, Vincent, *Hélène Desmaroux* (Poètes d'Aujourd'hui; Seghers, Paris, 1968)

Pia, Pascal, *Apollinaire par lui-même* (Ecrivains de Toujours; Seuil, Paris, 1957)

Polizzotti, Mark, *Revolution of the Mind: The Life of André Breton* (Bloomsbury, London, 1995)

Richardson, John, *A Life of Picasso, Vol. 2: 1907–1917: The Painter of Modern Life*, with the collaboration of Marilyn McCully (Jonathan Cape, London, 1996)

Sachs, Maurice, *Le Sabbat: Souvenirs d'une jeunesse orageuse* (Corrêa, Paris, 1946)

Savinio, Alberto [Andrea de Chirico], *Casa 'La Vita'* (Bompiani, Milan, 1943; Adelphi Edizione, Milan, 1995); *Hermaphrodito e altri romanzi*, edited by Alessandro Tinterri (Adelphi, Milan, 1995; title story first published 1918); *Infanzia di Nivasio Dolcemare* (Mondadori, Rome 1941), translated by Richard Pevear as *The Childhood of Nivasio Dolcemare*, introduced by Dore Ashton (Quartet, London, 1994); *Tutta la vita* (Bompiani, Milan, 1953)

Shattuck, Roger, *The Banquet Years: The Arts in France 1885–1918* (Faber and Faber, London, 1959); *The Innocent Eye: On Modern Literature and the Arts* (Farrar, Straus, and Giroux, New York, 1984)

Sorrell, Walter, *The Duality of Vision: Genius and Universality in the Arts* (Thames and Hudson, London, 1974)

Tisdall, Caroline and Angelo Bossola, *Futurism* (Thames and Hudson, London, 1977)

Waldberg, Patrick, *Surrealism* (Thames and Hudson, London, 1965)

Weininger, Otto, *Sex and Society*, authorized translation from the 6th German edn (Heinemann, London, 1906)

Index